D1796854

A CEMETERY IN MUNICH

If it comforts you, the Dane said, the grass will grow on the bombsites and the children will play with rag balls among broken masonry. The wind will disperse the fallout, if there is a fallout. . .

France has voted communist; Italy has voted communist. Russian tanks have come up to ten kilometres from the West German frontier.

And a quiet young NATO employee in Brussels selects this moment to vanish. For years, he's been copying classified papers and now he wants an auction for them. The bidders: East and West.

But the Dane, the distant manipulator, isn't exactly bidding. He sets a German to find him — a German to find a German; and an Englishman to make sure he doesn't kill him. . .

A CEMETERY
IN MUNICH

by

CHRISTOPHER HILTON

ROBERT HALE · LONDON

ISBN 0 7091 7481 0

Robert Hale Limited
Clerkenwell House
Clerkenwell Green
London, EC1R OHT

Photoset by Cahill Printers Limited, Dublin 3 and printed in
Great Britain by Redwood Burn Limited, Trowbridge & Esher

PREFACE

Two suppositions:

That the government of the United States of America decides — in great and laboured secrecy, no doubt — that the 7,000 nuclear weapons they deploy in Western Europe will be used only if there is an attack upon the American mainland. In other words, Detroit must not be placed in the front line, merely because somebody is firing missiles at Dusseldorf. This may seem fanciful and illogical; perhaps it is. It certainly goes against every public utterance of every American politician capable of making such decisions. But it is a conclusion reached by General de Gaulle, a decade and more ago.

That the people of Italy elect — democratically, properly, and legally — a communist government. As I write this, they have the largest communist party in Western Europe and seem perfectly capable of doing it. Second, that the people of France — second largest communist party — do the same. Not exactly the domino theory, but something like that. When this has happened, communism, in one form or another, will have control of territory from the Baltic in the north to the Adriatic; along the Mediterranean coast to the frontier of Spain, and all the way up the Atlantic to Dunkirk: A horse shoe in shape, and fashioned in gun-metal.

One observation:

That, as senior NATO officials remind us, the Russians already have far more men and weapons in Europe, facing west, than they could possibly require, if their objectives were purely defensive . . .

THE FIRST WEEK:
GESTURES IN THE DARK

SUNDAY

The searchlights were on.

Clark lay on his stomach in the long grass, his elbows dug into the ground and forming a tripod for the black binoculars which he trained on the frontier a thousand yards away.

Dusk, and a Godless January afternoon drowning slowly in the rain which raked the pine trees up the hillside; the mists of evening were rising in shifting layers, drifting towards the cattle who stood grouped near the stone wall at the far end of the field behind him, gazing, mute and suspicious, towards the point where he lay.

He was very wet. Already he had had to wipe both lenses of the binoculars with his handkerchief. Now he did so again, with the care and yet absent, circular motion of a man cleaning his spectacles; pressed the handkerchief back into his trouser pocket and looked toward the frontier once more. The wooden posts were ranged in a line across the field, at intervals of thirty metres, to mark the East German boundary. Each post had a yellow metal disk — embossed like a coat of arms, with the shape of a compass and a sheaf of wheat stamped onto it — nailed near its top. Twenty metres behind that, the wire itself, four metres high and supported by concrete posts; then the strip of naked brown earth behind the wire where the mines were sunk; then the narrow patrol road for the jeeps; then the ranks of tall lamp standards, their stems curving forward at their summits as if they sought to stoop. Each held a yellow light, and the area up to the wire and immediately beyond was drawn in perfect illumination: There was no shadow.

Clark swivelled his body and focussed on the watch-tower. It lay almost at the summit of the hill, behind the wire and in the middle of the cleared strip through the pine trees: An ugly, square cabin of re-inforced concrete supported by four stilts; an upraised pill-box with a slit in each wall. The searchlights were housed within it. Their beams poured from two of the slits, following mechanical courses along the wire: Now dipping and running across the patrol road, licking it; now rising, probing into the night sky. A Vopo came briefly to one of the slits and stood, a sharp, military silhouette. Clark could see his iron helmet, low over the ears for protection and shaped as if it had been moulded to the head.

They're bored, Clark thought, bored out of whatever brains they've got; they must be, five hours on, five hours off, surveying nothing except the static frontier, the unvarying courses of the searchlights and beyond, on the western tide, the unbroken darkness. He let go the binoculars and they hung, by the strap. He checked the time. 4.48. He'd stay a few moments, until night had fallen. He was almost certainly out of sight, but he was a cautious man and he wouldn't take any chances now.

Damn this rain, he thought: A wretched, rotten day, a typical Sunday, empty and as cold as a Catholic church, the candles all extinguished.

He waited another twenty minutes and began the long crawl back.

He rose and walked only when he was close to the gate. Simpson and Craig were in the car off the unkept road from Hohegeiss, an abandoned track between two tall hedges, its surface scarred by potholes. Nobody cared. Half a mile to the east, the wire crudely bisected it, and it was useless now, going nowhere: A remnant of the war, the consequences of a line drawn on a map thirty years before.

Hohegeiss: Clark had thought a lot about the village while he lay in the field: It was only a hamlet, some old houses gathered round a cobbled square, their angled, tiled rooftops falling together and seeming to support each other; a pump in the middle of the square, a decorative thing which probably hadn't drawn water for half a century and was not painted black. A stone stand had been constructed around it, encircled by empty flower-beds.

Hohegeiss: It was only big enough to carry three shops and a bureau of agricultural credit. Clark had stopped in the square because Simpson wanted to buy cigarettes. One of the shops had closed down in a hurry. Cardboard boxes were scattered across the bare, linoleum floor; a heap of tins, fruit and meats and soups, had been stacked in a corner: Too heavy to bear away. Down one of the side-roads, a family were moving out. They must have hired the white van. The father and teenage daughter were lifting small pieces of furniture into it. The mother, a spreading, fattened woman, stood by the opened front door, clutching two heavy suitcases. Neighbours watched from their windows. The house two doors away was unoccupied, curtains taken down, lightbulbs unscrewed. They'd gone, too.

Clark had parked near the bureau of credit and, while Simpson was away, examined the notice board — a varnished wooden frame with a glass front — fixed to the wall next to it. The interior was dominated by a large, official decree: A printed message with a space for the name of the town to be written by hand.

FELLOW GERMANS! FELLOW CITIZENS OF HOHEGISS! WE PLEDGE OURSELVES TO REMAIN CALM DURING THE PRESENT EMERGENCY. WE WILL NOT BE ALARMED BY THE RUMOUR-MONGERS, OR SUBVERSIVES SEEKING TO SPREAD CONFUSION. WE ALL KNOW THAT THE AMERICAN SHIELD WILL PROTECT US, AND THE BUNDESWEHR! AND WE STATE THAT GERMANS WILL NOT SHOOT AT GERMANS!

(signed) Alfred Gross, Regierungsprasident, Braunschweig.

(signed) Otto Kremer, Stadtdirektor, Braunlage.

That had been the afternoon. Now, as he walked down the lane, Clark saw the outline of the car and the two men inside it. He opened the door. Simpson sat in the back, wearing a raincoat and smoking; Craig in the passenger seat in the front, encased in some light-blue dungarees. He looked like a garage mechanic.

"Know what?" Craig said when Clark was back inside the car. "That village back there. The Krauts are moving out. Got the wind up. We've been talking about it, while you've been away." He was a short, furtive little Londoner; a ferret of a man, born and bred in the East End, in a red-brick tenement off the Mile End Road, where you had to be sharp to get through; he had restless eyes which moved between the morose, the distrustful and the eager. "No guts," he said conclusively, "no bottle at all. The bastards are running away."

5.23.

"We'll move in a moment," Clark said. "You both know what to do, so I don't propose to go through the whole thing again. Unless you have any questions."

"You asked us that before," Craig said.

"I meant any further questions," Clark replied heavily. Major Clark, ill at ease in civilian clothing; a man of average height, geometrically created for the British battledress because there was a solid symmetry to his shoulders; a small, tufted moustache; receding hair habitually camouflaged beneath the peaked service cap and now exposed, threadbare as an old carpet; a square, heavy face, the texture of the skin florid. He wore an overcoat which he must have harboured all these years without finding the occasion to put it on. Its shoulders were creased by suspension on a coat hanger. It smelt distantly of neglect and carried the soft, feminine odour of mothballs.

"Still don't fancy the Vz58," Craig said. "Czech rubbish. They jam. You know that?"

Clark was looking along the road. There had been an urgency about the briefing, two days before. A man he hadn't seen before had come; a tall man, a German; a man sure of himself; a man who had given just so much information and no more. We must have Czech rifles, the man had said, because if they retrieve the ammunition, they can't prove anything.

"Those Vz58s are as delicate as lawn-mowers," Craig went on. "You don't squeeze, you push." He nodded his head. He might have been conducting a conversation entirely with himself. "Me, I like the good old Lee Enfield, Mark One for preference. Lovely feel, like a woman. And that 7.62 calibre. Handsome, that rifle, bleeding handsome."

"I've been reading a book," Simpson said suddenly and without warning. He was from the north, a thick-set, reliable man — the kind you entrust with your life savings and don't worry. He had the crew cut of a regular soldier. "It's by an American, and it's called: Aspects of Society." He grunted. "He says things like this shouldn't happen."

Craig was half-indignant, half-mocking. He, too, was looking out along the lane, strewn with manure which had fallen from a trailer on its way to the fields. "Aspects of society." He mocked, just in the repetition of the title. By his intonation, each of the three words became dismembered and grotesque. "That's your trouble," he said, "you think too much."

The moon was up, naked and alone, clear enough to be mottled white, a lonely outline away to the right. The rain had gone. "I was hoping for cloud," Clark said. "Never mind. The mist will help."

5.41.

"Check watches," Clark said. "5.41, going on 5.42. Simpson, you don't start until Craig already has. Don't even let that index finger of yours twitch. All right?"

Simpson murmured something; it must have been assent.

Both the rifles were in a golf bag in the boot. Clark drew them out of it and handed each man the ammunition, three metal clips, crescent-shaped and deep green, almost khaki. In silence, he pressed the boot lit down until it was closed and secured the lock; toured the car, checking that the doors were secured, too.

They walked along the lane in single file, Clark leading. He unravelled the chain on the gate, pushed the gate back, and they went through. They were in mud, the mud that the cows had churned, standing aimlessly by the gate; the grooves that their hooves had cut were filled with water. Half way across the field, when they could see the searchlights, Clark motioned to Simpson, who broke away, going left, in a crouched position, rifle tucked in at his side.

Clark sensed the cattle close by; but they did not move. They must have been there somewhere, craggy, prehensile heads peering stupidly into the folds of greying, whitening mist.

He signalled with his hand held flat and parallel to the ground, moving it downward; both he and Craig sank into the grass. Then they began to crawl.

"This bleeding grass is wet," Craig hissed.

When they stopped, they were close to the pine trees. Clark fumbled for the binocular case, dragging along on the strap at his side, unclipped it, took out the binoculars and surveyed the wire. It was a hundred and fifty yards away. They crawled forward again, the grass brushing at their faces. At seventy-five yards, they stopped again.

5.59.

They were on the incline, close by the perimeter of the trees. Pine-cones lay underfoot, too moist to crackle.

"Here," Clark said, very softly. He had the binoculars out again, facing them onto the watchtower. Craig had the rifle in his hands and was fitting the silencer to its barrel, a twisting of the wrist once, twice, three times until the thin, perforated metal cylinder was tight. He tugged at it to make sure, then, when he was perfectly satisfied, brought a clip of ammunition out of his trouser pocket and pressed it into the aperture under the rifle and just in front of the trigger-guard. "The range is all right," he said, a professional evaluation. He'd been trained as a sniper; and they all said it: He's a bloody good shot. He'd make Roy Rogers look like an amateur.

He lay beside Clark, smoothing the grass down in front of him with his left hand. When he had finished that, and it lay in a pleated matt, he aligned himself — a series of small, sharp jerks of the body — until he was directly facing the watchtower; held the posture for a long moment, as if he was verifying some factor hidden from any but a specialist with a rifle, contracting and holding himself absolutely motionless. "I thought the elevation might be tricky," he observed. "It's not. Thank Christ for that."

6.04.

"Eleven minutes," Clark said. "Relax. Distract yourself. Think about birds." He laughed, but the pitch of it was false. He was nervous.

Craig went slack, lying face down in the grass. The rifle was next to him, his hand wrapped around the mechanical part to protect it from the wet. He was beginning to concentrate. The other hand stroked the butt of the rifle, exploring the sequence of grooves cut into the wood for grip.

Now he was calculating the glare of the searchlights, the angle of movement at their base; how quickly he could alter his position to take the lamps on the standards. Eleven of them.

"They'll call the jeep on the emergency phone," Clark said after a long time. "It will take a minimum of three minutes to get here. We've checked that."

Craig didn't hear; or, if he did, he made no observation. That wasn't his problem. Only the lights.

"The jeep is stationed a kilometre away," Clark said. "It

patrols sporadically, mostly going in the other direction: South. They must think the're more vulnerable down there." He needed to talk. 6.09. "Blasted French" he said. "All this is their damn fault. They all go and vote socialist with nice, smiling candidates buttering them up — and they wake up from their bloody fornicating to find they've got themselves a communist government with all the trappings. I bet a few of them choked over their continental breakfasts when they realised that. How can they be that stupid?"

"Just foreigners," Craig said without enthusiasm, the insular contempt of the English which seemed, in times of stress, perfectly legitimate.

"Simpson must be in position now." Clark's coat was sodden, and the water had seeped into the material, leaving it stained and discoloured. "A good man, that. A reliable man. I don't know him well, but I can sense it."

"Too serious. He reads those books all the time. He's teaching himself some dead language: Sanscrit or Ancient Greek or something. Every morning when he shaves, he has a dictionary propped up in front of the mirror and he learns five new words. The first morning when I heard him, I thought he was being sick. The noises he makes in his throat, getting those bleeding words out."

6.12.

"I hope Echtmann is ready. If not, God help us all. . . ." Clark thought suddenly of Hohegeiss, and the decree, and the notices bordering it: For your haircut, visit Leonard, Bauerstrasse. Jesus is coming — prepare yourself. Beware black ice on the autobahns. The sane world, a kilometre and a half away; mortgages and clinics and sleeping pills; timetables and plumbing which worked; and white removal vans.

6.13.

"Stand to," Clark said. "I don't mean stand up, I mean prepare yourself." His lips were dry and he scoured them with his tongue to coat them in moisture. He lifted the binoculars again, observed the mist which seemed to gather around the distant lamp standards. "Echtmann won't move until all the lights are out. That was the understanding. That was the promise."

Craig positioned himself in the classic shape: The left elbow against the ground, supporting the rifle half way down the barrel; the right looping round it to allow the fingers to spread within the trigger guard, the index finger on the trigger itself.

6.14. The seconds were important now. Echtmann had been told 6.15 precisely; not a minute either side; but 6.15.

"If I say stop firing, stop firing," Clark said. It must have been on his mind: The need to be in control of a fluid, developing situation when anything could happen. The whole thing was a risk. It was the urgency which had compelled them to it. The man who had briefed him had been hard about that. It's all arranged, he had said. We have to get him across. The conventional stuff, hiding in lorries and so on, is out. No time for that.

He had the binoculars up still.

The searchlights moved away, silently tracking a far section of the wire.

"Now." His voice was taut. He saw the rifle recoil against Craig's shoulder. He drew the binoculars to his eyes. The searchlight went out immediately, and they could both hear glass breaking. Craig had raised the barrel of the rifle and began to pick off the lamps, in a cadence, one after another. A coconut shy at the fair, Clark thought jubilantly. He could smell cordite. The spent cartridges were spewed back, one at a time, into the grass. Craig hesitated at number seven, emptied three shots into it and muttered a reproach to himself before it was extinguished; then moved on. Simpson had begun on the other side of the watchtower almost at the same time; had taken his searchlight first, and was now working his way along the lamps.

They all heard a German voice, shocked and angry, inside the tower, shouting into a telephone and, at both the side slits, torches came on, hand held, probing fearfully into the darkened night.

Clark saw, through the binoculars, Echtmann rise like a rabbit from beyond the lamps, the girl behind him; saw them both run across the patrol road and onto the mined strip, their feet bare because somebody in Brussels was sure that the pressure of bare feet was negligible, and the mines wouldn't be activated; saw that he was in jeans and a pullover, the pallid beam from one of the torches straining to keep him in focus; the girl was all in his shadow, long skirt flapping frantically at her ankles.

Echtmann was running dead straight.

The single shot from the watchtower — without reasonance, without echo — which brought him down, hands clutching his left leg, must have been a fluke. A pistol — any pistol — was completely inaccurate over twenty yards. Clark knew that. Craig knew that. Too bad.

The girl came on, under her own impetus, leaving Echtmann where he had fallen; came safely over the mined strip, reached the wire, the torch probing for her, and began to climb, her fingers hooking into the gaps in the mesh.

Clark stood up and stumbled forward, in the grass, arms outstretched.

Craig, unbidden, began to fire at the watchtower, shot after shot, until the magazine was empty. With crisp, practiced movements, he disengaged the empty clip, let it drop into the grass, clipped in another one and resumed.

The girl had clambered to the top of the wire and had one leg over. She lost her balance and fell forward onto the western side. Clark called out, in English: "Run towards me." The staves of the boundary were still twenty metres away, the Vopos could still shoot at her.

Clark lifted the binoculars. Echtmann was on the edge of the patrol road, twisting and turning from side to side; but not even crawling, crippled, forward onto the mined strip. The torch beam moved back and held him, like a creature paralysed in the headlights of a car. His forehead was moist, the thick, black hair pressed down onto the skin by his own sweat. A little blood, from below the knee, had seeped onto the roadway; thick enough to glisten in the torchlight.

"Kill him," Clark called back.

Craig adjusted the barrel; saw in the round sight above the barrel — an eyepiece, bisected by two crossing black lines, one vertical, one horiztontal — Echtmann's face, rocking without control; saw, momentarily, his fevered eyes, half-raised; pressed the trigger, a pressure as gentle as coaxing milk from a baby's bottle; felt the remote, umbilical cord between the weapon and the figure on the roadway; waited without needing to press the trigger again — waited until blood was now flowing down Echtmann's forehead and he lay still.

Clark was excited. "If they fire at me, hammer that watchtower. I'm going to get the girl." He shouted it, abandoning caution. He went down the dip in the field, and was lost. Craig covered the watchtower, but he knew — the flickering, momentary comprehension of the city-dweller raised on differing atmospheres — that it was all over.

When Clark came back, she was crying.

Craig said: "I'm sorry, dear. If I'd known the torches were so powerful. . . ."

The jeep came along the road on the far side of the wire and two Vopos jumped from it. They left the engine running and ran towards the watchtower.

"Erik is dead," the girl said. She turned and gazed to the east; through the mesh to the unmoving, crumpled body, one arm splayed outward, the back of the motionless hand brushing the tarmac; the other loosened about the knee, and the leg doubled beneath the body.

Clark stood near her, unsure whether to comfort her openly; or whether, by his proximity, that might be comfort in itself.

"We might as well walk back," Craig said pointedly. "It's a bit bloody late for the crawling."

SUNDAY, MIDNIGHT

Clark stood by the window of the nissen hut, looking out across the camp: the parade ground, with the white lines of a handball area painted around it, stretched away to the other group of huts and, looming behind that, the laundry chimney. A solitary sentry, sitting on a bench outside the brick gatehouse, was smoking furtively, half concealed behind a conifer bush. It was raining again, the angular, slanted rain which stings the naked skin. Clark watched the patterns of it, dribbling down the windowpane in rivulets, transluscent in the camp lights.

"Don't hurry drinking the tea," Clarke said. He had placed his overcoat across the desk and one of the arms hung flat and limp over the front of it. A little of the rainwater, the residue of the long grass, dripped insistently from the wrist, into a plump little pool on the floorboards.

The girl was fair and pretty in an ordinary way; possibly — probably — still a teenager. Her hair was wet and clung to her head behind her ears as if she had just emerged from a shower. She sat on the thin, wooden chair by Clark's desk, nursing the mug. A slogan had been painted around it: Fifty Fifth Armoured, Rugby tour, 1959, but her long fingers were wreathed about the circumference, masking whole segments of the words. Her eyes were veined red. Concussion, Clark thought. Delayed shock. Whatever they call it. Like a car crash. She's gone to pieces.

The sentry cast down the cigarette butt, ground it with his

boot, exhaled the last, strained, greyed smoke — the colour of industrial effluent — turned up his battledress collar, and stood.

Clark let the lace curtains fall back together and turned to her. She doesn't know we killed Echtmann, she was confused and running, she couldn't deduce the direction of the shot. She'll think it was the Vopos. She's been conditioned to hate them, to blame them. She must never know.

"He wanted us to be married in Bamberg," she said, very softly, like a bird with a broken wing, alive but the future destroyed. "He carried a postcard of the big church there. I can't think where he got it from. He told me he had some relatives nearby. He was to get a job as a mechanic. He promised we would have such a fine wedding." She began to cry again, letting the tears run freely down her face, her hands never leaving the warmth of the mug. Just then, Clark realised stupidly that she hadn't been able to bring over a handbag, a handkerchief; nothing. "I wish I had died out there with him. I wish. . . ." The thinned voice faded, ashamed of its own weakness; seeking to bury the weakness in silence. She wore a thin coat; a dress in a floral pattern, ravaged by the rain and the crouching on the other side. The hem must have trailed in the grass, soaked by the rain; a party dress, her best; she'd have wanted to bring that with her and the only way was to wear it. Her feet were bare, the toes white.

She placed the mug on the floor and began to take off the engagement ring.

"I'm terribly sorry," Clark said, forcing a measure of diffidence which was strained. "But I have to ask you some questions. It is very important, or else it could have waited." He wanted to excuse himself, to prove, even to her, that it was human; and, in a remote way, that life was better here, on the western side. He went behind the desk, pushed the coat to one side, and produced a notebook, each page ruled in feint, green lines up and across, in the Continental way.

"It's all going to happen," she said in a vague way. "Erik told me, over and over again, these last few weeks. They have started pulling people back from the frontier to a depth of twenty kilometres. Whole villages, men, women and children, even babies. They take them across country, further east: To what they call hospitality centres. That's what they call them." Her eyes scanned the joints between the floorboards, as if she might have been seeking solace there; they were the deadened eyes of the shocked, seeing in one dimension rather than the three. "I know the truth. They are putting families into huts and old aircraft hangars and outhouses used to keep animals. Pig-sties."

Clark fumbled in an unseen drawer and lifted out a hip-size bottle of Scotch; unscrewed the silver cap, placed that on the desk, and proffered it towards her. "I don't drink," she said decisively, "but thank you for being so kind."

He drank himself, letting the acidity bite at the back of his throat. "It's the troop movements I must have," he said. "It's the details, especially the insignias on their shoulder bands. Even if you can only remember the pattern of colours, the reds or the whites or the blues."

"They started coming two weeks ago," she began. The engagement ring had been slipped off, and she placed it with great care in her coat pocket. "Erik made many enquiries for you. He was a good worker — for you. He took many risks. You could hardly be expected to understand. I loved him, I did not want to see him die on a roadway, with only a torch shining in his face. . . ." She dabbed her eyes with the sleeve of the coat, instinct or to preserve appearances. It didn't matter which. "It was always Russians, never East Germans. And always at night, under the cover of the darkness. Columns of them, in lorries. They are billeted now in the villages which the people have been moved out of; animals, those soldiers. I do not think they even know how to use toilets."

"Which Russians? Did Erik find out?" Clark — seated at the desk, the biro suspended over the notebook. He had written nothing.

She shrugged. "Near us, from Halberstadt to Nordhausen, infantry and tanks. The infantry all had their polushbki. Perhaps you do not understand Russian. She looked at him, waiting for the gesture which would tell her that he did not understand.

"I do not suppose you speak Russian. We speak a little. It is taught in all the schools, for a minimum of three years. Polushubok are sheepskin coats. In our sector, they were the Second Guards Army, and they had come by train from Vilnius to Berlin; then by lorry. Each of the lorries towed a katyush mortar, or a field gun of some kind. There was a curfew and a strict blackout, but when Erik heard them passing, he stood by the window watching. As you did, when I first came in here. It was so strange that they came through the centre of the town, not round it. That would have been much more sensible, no? It was that which made Erik think it was very serious."

"How many lorries?" Clark had begun to write, a hasty, ill-shaped series of notes. These cheap biros were wrong for decent handwriting; that, and the sporadic inkflow. You couldn't get a flourish with them, just mean little characters which looked like a scribble.

"Too many to count. One night, the procession — the convoy — lasted almost one hour."

"And. . . ."

"And four days ago, they started coming again. Ukranians, also in lorries. After midnight. The lorries towed missiles, draped in camouflage nets. You could still see the shapes, and the fins at the end."

"How long were the rockets . . . the missiles?"

She shrugged again. "It was dark. I've told you: There was a curfew and a blackout. Maybe thirty metres, maybe more. I

was very frightened." She had begun to compose herself
again; her hair was drying out, and now looked as pleated as
the grass which Craig had smoothed before him. "We heard
that others were taking up positions in the north, in Stendal
and Schwerin. I don't know about nearer the Baltic. We
didn't hear. Nor in the south, in the Dresden-Leipzig axis."

"It's late," Clark said. She wondered, cynically, whether he
had said that because the information she was furnishing was
useless, or whether he was genuinely concerned. "After
midnight. I think you ought to get some sleep. Somebody else
will come to see you in the morning, to go through it all in
much more detail." Clark, preparing the ground in spite of
her suffering; Clark, keeping all those options open.

"What is to happen to me?" She was an orphan now,
trapped and held in the no-man's land between east and west.
Perhaps she sensed that Clark hadn't wanted her to come
over; had said, mutedly, at the briefing, that the girl
complicated the whole thing. But Echtmann had insisted:
Both of us or nothing at all. Both of us, or you can get
stuffed. He'd even known enough English to use exactly that
phrase. Had, apparently, employed it with relish.

"Don't you worry," Clark said. "Everything will be taken
care of." Again the strained diffidence, the bogus assurance.
He didn't know what was going to happen to the girl. They
hadn't told him about that. A human being before him, and
nothing he could do but tell lies. She wasn't so innocent. She
would understand his position: The honest Englishman,
awkward, doing his best, doing his duty, doing what they had
told him. Always the *They*. It as no kind of excuse; but it was
no time for introspection or shallow philosophy, based on
broken people. Sometimes he hated himself for being this
callous, and he knew that circumstances would never
condone it; he'd tried to lose himself in the *They*, the right of
the machine to make its own judgements, its own
calculations, demand its own sacrifices; but he wasn't like

that; although he suspected that the machine was.

"I want to see a priest." She was looking up at him, meek and tortured; prepared that he might be surprised, because she was so young, and her country had decreed atheism and enforced it.

"Now?"

"Now. If this is possible. I understand the lateness of the hour, but. . . ."

So bloody polite. It might have touched Clark, that, if he hadn't had a hard night himself, and hadn't ordered a British soldier to shoot a fallen civilian — a civilian who was on his side — through the wire. Of course that did not constitute murder, not in any court of conscience. He'd told himself that a dozen times on the drive back to the camp, the girl in the front passenger seat, and Simpson and Craig in the back, none of them saying anything. Clark had driven with exaggerated care, wondering what would have happened if a lorry had hit them, and they'd all been killed. Who would have sorted it out?

The rain beat against the room of the nissen hut. Why in hell didn't it stop, just for a few minutes?

"All right," Clark said. He put the overcoat laboriously back on. "Just stay here." He looked at her again as he reached the doors: The flecks of mud on the floral dress, the bare legs, the naked feet; the discarded mug on the floor. He thought of Echtmann, writhing and writhing and writhing, contorting himself; and she, running to the wire, away from him, with no moment to turn and see that he had been hit.

Clark walked briskly towards the parade ground, the rain in his face. The priest was asleep in one of the nissen huts; he came nervously to the door when Clark knocked, a thin, diminutive man with callow skin, as if he had hidden from daylight all his life, a hairless, nocturnal mole.

"There is a young girl in my office," Clark said. "She came across tonight. Her fiance was killed by the Vopos. She's in a bit of a state. She wants you."

The priest went noiselessly away to dress. One thing about these Catholics, Clark thought: They really believe it. No complaint, no insinuation about the time and the weather. No muted suggestion that it would be inconvenient. Strange. The girl knew perfectly well that the priest would react like that.

They walked back together, side by side, in silence, the priest wearing a grey raincoat with a belt which he hadn't bothered to secure at the buckle. As they went into the office, the girl raised her eyes. She had not moved from the chair, as if to do so might constitute trespass. The priest smiled, a watery, pathetic smile, the trade mark of doctors who seek to reassure before they enquire what is wrong; a smile healing to the believer, repugnant to the rest. Clark wasn't a believer at all, at least not in the formal sense: The ritual of organised religion was quaint and harmless, but mumbo-jumbo for all that. On official forms, he habitually wrote: Church of England in the compartment marked FAITH — but that was just to keep them all at bay.

"Leave us alone," the priest said evenly, neither a request nor an instruction but a simple, humble statement to which there could be no denial.

Clark wandered over to the night operations room, a square, brick building secluded down a passage between two huts at the edge of the parade ground. Two men were on duty, a sergeant and a private, sitting at a bench with headphones covering their ears and facing khaki-coloured receivers.

"Anything?" Clark asked. He had a right to be in the room. Military intelligence. Others didn't, and were turned away, never mind their rank.

The sergeant pulled down the earphones so they hung like a scarf round his neck. "Movements," he said conclusively. His sleeves were rolled up to the elbows, and a tattoo was enscribed on each forearm: Boogie Street on the left, Singapore on the right. He was masticating chewing gum. A half-finished cigarette burned alone in a metal ashtray beside him. "They're moving the whole time. Want to listen?" Clark shook his head.

The map was laid on the bench between the operators — an ordnance survey map, curiously, available anywhere. A tobacco tin was full of black marking pins.

"We're not putting those in any more," the sergeant said. "Waste of our time. There are too many tanks over there, and too much movement. The tank crews are not even bothering to talk in code." He heard a sound, lifted the headphones and adjusted them to his ears, using both hands at once. "As a pattern, they're coming forward to within ten kilometres of the frontier, then stopping; they must be in the fields. The roads could never cope with them. When they're in position, they just halt and stop transmitting. God knows what they do after that. Silence means we know when they've arrived. Then we start on the next bloody lot. I didn't know there were that many tanks anywhere."

Clark was leaning forward, over the map. "Where are they?"

The sergeant, lip-reading, disengaged the headphones and ran his finger down the map. "Here . . . and here . . . and here. Those are the main concentrations. We locate them when they come over the Bode river. Their technicians think the bridge at Oschersleben isn't strong enough. But they haven't had time to reinforce it, see? We pick them up as they approach the bridge. It's like a funnel. We track them as they disperse when they're across. It's all organised. . . ."

When Clark returned to his office, he sensed that the girl had been crying again.

"She needs sleep," the priest observed, seeming

uncomfortable with the third person in the room. "I telephoned the matron. She has arranged a bed in the hospital. Behind screens for privacy. She assured me of that. Otherwise the girl would be in amongst the men. I also asked her to try and find a pair of shoes, size $5\frac{1}{2}$."

They left her at the hospital. Most of the beds were empty.

"She confessed," the priest said, as they walked away. "I'm not supposed to say that, not even that; but she did. She needed the confession. I could hardly help her at all." He walked quickly, because he was so thin and carried so little weight. "She is sure there is going to be another war. She thinks that, when they come from the east, they will find her and do terrible things to her. She says they are so strong, so many thousands of them, who don't reason and don't think, but just advance, regardless of casualties. . . ."

Half an hour later, when Clark had been to the night operations room again and was returning to his quarters, he noticed a light in the nave of the small, red-brick chapel. The studded door was open, and he went in.

Empty pews, and a slate, stone aisle leading to the altar. That was cloaked in red cloth — it must have been velvet — with the silver crucifix placed upon it and a newly-lighted candle at either side of it.

Clark hesitated; went further in. Even from where he stood, at the back, he could see the priest knelt on the second of the three steps up the altar, his hands clasped together, his head bowed in supplication.

The shelves in the pews were heavy with hymn books; knee cushions were clipped to brass hooks.

"Please God," he heard the priest say, distinctly, but as if the words came from a detached being a great distance away, "please God, not again."

MONDAY

A blue Ford Cortina met Clark at the Gare du Quartier Leopold. The Aachen train had been a handful of minuutes late, and now Clark stood outside the station, searching for the chauffeur; found him, leaning against the bonnet of the car; showed him his plastic identification disc. The man looked at it without touching it, nodded distractedly, and got back into the car.

Early afternoon, and a darkened sky pressing down hard on the city of bureaucrats; heavy, running cloud was being pushed urgently by the wind and rain was in the air. To the north, the cloud was even lower and the rain must already be falling there.

He sat in the back of the Ford and reflected on the marque: Just large enough to get away with the chauffeur, just small enough to emphasise Clark's position. Actually, he hadn't expected a car at all, and was surprised when he was told there would be one there.

Brussels: He hadn't been there for ten years and, as the car moved away, he regarded it with the eye of a man searching for a measure of his own past. Seeping, faltering traffic, a lot of it bearing diplomatic number plates, struggled down steep, cobbled streets; a Gothic church on a mount, isolated by the circling vehicles, with an avenue of bare trees leading to the nave door and, nearby, a granite monument covered in graffitti; a hybrid city, with every street name in French and Flemish, the political compromise to placate, not enlighten;

an industrial city, webbed by fly-overs and half-completed viaducts removing the last, lingering assumptions of charm.

It was a place you came to for business; or to be buried.

They gained the inner ring road, reaching it up a curving slipway flanked by bushes. Heavy lorries ground forward in procession, Belgian, German, French and one or two Dutch with trailers, all obediently arranged in the nearside lane. The cars stayed away from them, as if by instinct. They were on the autoroute in twenty minutes. It had been laid in precast sections, and the car stuttered across the joints where the segments had been thrust together; did it with the rhythmic monotony of a train, crossing points. Seventeen or eighteen kilometres out into the country, Clark saw the livid green sign, set back onto the grass verge: NATO service area, next turning left. They descended lazily and came to an intersection beneath the autoroute. The noise of the lorries passing overhead persisted, like the distant echo of heavy artillery.

The driver had said nothing. Clark assumed he spoke no English. He wore a raincoat with a blue uniform beneath it. Clark had his battledress on, and a cumbersome khaki greatcoat over it. The beret suited him, tucked in just above the ears and no strand of hair visible.

A kilometre away, they turned onto a narrower road; passed a farm with a canal running beside it and a horse and foal in one corner of a field, wandering slowly.

The sign was precisely the same colour and height as the one on the autoroute had been: NATO service area. After that, a white sign about unauthorised personnel and, beside it, a sketch of a large dog informing, graphically, that the area was guarded.

Clark saw the first ring of perimeter wire long before they reached it; it reminded him of the East German frontier: The same elevation, the same supports. . . .

The driver halted in front of the red pole which lay, waist

high, across the road; waited patiently there, the engine breathing softly to itself, until the sentry had come forward from the brick guard house and had motioned for the car to advance a little.

The chauffeur drew up to the pole, and the sentry examined Clark's plastic disc with great care, his head thrusting directly into the car so that he might see Clark's face properly to match it with the photograph. He retained the disc, turned and walked stiffly back to the guardhouse and made a telephone call; returned, his boots clattering noisily on the surface of the road; handed the disc back and began to wind a lever at the end of the pole. It raised very slowly, and they went through, the chauffeur observing the 5 kph speed limit very precisely.

The gap between the perimeter wire and the inner ring of it was probably a hundred metres. The road was flanked by more urgent signs: Beware, mines.

The procedure at the second guardhouse was the same. While the ritual was being enacted, Clark looked ahead and saw the rows of concrete buildings, each submerged so that only four or five feet of them was visible; saw the humps in the ground, covered in grass, the strategic shapes of a headquarters; saw, away by some silver birch trees, a circular radar antennae moving silently. No building carried any marking save a number on a post, in the grass beside it.

The chauffeur stopped at number seventeen, waited until Clark was out, did a laboured three-point turn, and went away. Clark walked down a path, descended some stone steps which took him beneath a reinforced concrete awning; faced a metal door, with a slit for vision from the interior. There was no bell and, absurdly, for a moment he had no idea what to do. He rapped with his knuckles. A teenage girl came, in pullover and skirt.

"My name is Clark," he said. "Major Clark." She hesitated, leaving him outside like a vacuum cleaner salesman, awaiting a rejection. But he wasn't going to show the disc to her. And he thought — perhaps, quite unconsciously, he was gathering evidence — of the radio operator and the tanks so numerous they couldn't be counted, couldn't be plotted, couldn't even be allocated black marking pins on the choked map. And here. They'd sent a junior typist to meet him, a little creature just out of puberty. He went in and she closed the door behind him. Another girl sat at a desk, talking into a telephone and giggling.

They went down a corridor, all the doors closed, and buff, coconut matting underfoot, in a strip not wide enough to reach across the width of the corridor. The girl knocked at one of the doors, mumbled something — it might have been in French or Flemish or German or anything, because it was spoken in the thin, nervous voice of a girl like that — and held the door open for Clark to enter: A small, meagre office with no window and, consquently, no view, even of the grass, and a young man in uniform behind the desk.

"Major Clark," he said. "Good trip?" He skirted the desk and advanced, holding out a slender, white hand to be shaken. Clark gripped it firmly, and felt the nerve-tissues instinctively try to withdraw. They did say that, during the Russian Revolution, people had to hold their hands out to see if they were calloused; if they weren't, the owner of the hands had never done manual work and couldn't be a worker. Clark had another kind of test: The strength of the handshake. A man would shake hands hard, a real man, a soldier. This one was an administrator. "My name is Gorlish," he said. "I'm operational liaison." He smiled bleakly, as if he might have wished to apoligise for the position. "Cup of tea? They ship us the real thing. Tetley's Tea Bags. A concession for HQ. I am told the active camps in Germany are much more spartan."

Clark released the hand and it fall, limp, away from him. "No tea? Really?" Clark shook his head. And he wanted to say: What happens to you, sonny, if all those tanks start to roll? They'd be here in a day and a half, maybe less, if they were driven through the night. Got your Sabena airline ticket for London ready, just as a contingency of course, but still tucked discreetly in one of those drawers in the desk? Got your personal effects packed and labelled, just in case? A tactical withdrawal by the British liaison officer, who has influenza. Gorlish gazed at him, uncertain what to say; he regarded Clark as he would have done an Ancient Briton, smeared with paint and holding a spear. "The Old Man wants to see you. Don't know why." They stood a yard apart. "I have the Devil's own job getting at him myself, for important things." Clark removed the beret, rolled it up and placed it in his greatcoat pocket; smoothed his hair back with the palm of his right hand. Gorlish said: "He speaks perfect English, by the way. Quite perfect. He has mastered even the idiomatic expressions. He did four years in London, during the war. If you make any grammatical errors, he will correct them. Not that you will, of course." The bleak smile again, lost somewhere between arrogance and Oliver asking for just a little more soup." I must telephone down and see if he's free."

When that was done, they walked together into the corridor, along it, away from the secretaries, to a lift. Gorlish pressed the summon button, and they waited, in awkward silence. They went in. Five floors down. They were in another corridor which smelt of mildew and damp. "You're lucky to get down here at all," Gorlish observed. "Most don't." They had begun to walk forward. "The Old Man can be hard when he wants." Another door, hermettrically sealed with rubber edging. "You'll find out, major." Gorlish knocked, hesitated, opened it at the word of command from within, and said simply: "In you go."

He went in alone.

"Do close the door behind you." The voice was easy and cultivated but still bore Nordic traces, the off-key formulation of the sounds which could never be eradicated. The intonation on the *do* was perfect. Clark pushed at the door, and was surprised it moved back so easily, closed so firmly. He looked round. This was no kind of office: It was a monk's cell. The walls had been made of stone blocks, coated in distemper. The apparatus of air-conditioning clung, high up in one corner, near the ceiling, with in-flow and out-flow valves, a noiseless machine. A bare, green metal desk faced him. The Dane sat in a chair behind it. One chair had been placed before it, for Clark. There was nothing else in the room, except two telephones — one black, one red — on the desk.

"Do sit down and make yourself comfortable." He might have been an Oxford tutor, dispensing intimate advice and — perhaps — a glass of sherry.

Clark unloosened the buttons of the greatcoat and sat. Then he surveyed the Dane: A man of sixty, a thinned, trim man of average height with a sharp face and pure white hair, white as the foam which breaks across the rocks and ebbs away; he had eyes which said: I remember you, I know you, we have met before; perhaps only once before. You do not expect me to remember you, because of what I am and the countless faces which pass before me; but yours I remember. Perhaps that is why I am what I am, and I hold the position I hold. Your mannerisms do not surprise me; they have not changed.

He had eyes which were almost green, the shading of turbulent seas at dusk. The lips of the mouth were thin and dry and autocratic, the product of deliberate selection — not chance breeding — over generations.

The hands were thin, also, and if they had ever done any kind of manual work, the marks of it had long since gone. The Dane would have failed the Russian test easily. Blue veins were threaded across the back of them like intricate lacework; they protruded above the level of the skin, linear

welts. He wore a light blue uniform, but a different texture to
that of the chauffeur; and no medals, no shoulder bands; a
cream shirt and a navy blue tie knotted in what they used to
call a half-Windsor.

"I have read your report," he said. "It was relayed here by
telex this morning." One of his front teeth had been capped
near its base, in pure gold. "Your report . . ." and he
gesticulated, implying that the report was in close proximity
and, perhaps, very valuable; though not in this room. "The
interrogation of the girl who came across. The preliminary
interrogation of the girl who came across. She knew very
little. Echtmann was most prudent in not divulging it to her.
In the end, because she survived and he did not, that worked
against us. A pity."

Clark sat, pressing the chair back away from the desk so
that there was room for his legs. "The girl wanted to go back
to the wire this morning and lay a wreath against it, for
Echtmann, I refused her permission. It would have been like
admitting . . ." Clark leant forward, and he was over the desk,
stooping across it, the metal of its surface cold against his
wrists. "We killed Echtmann. I gave that order."

The Dane had not moved. His hands were now below the
desk and unseen; his shoulders were still. "I heard she
confessed to a priest. You are not required to do the same,
major. . . ."

Clark adjusted himself back into the chair.

"It was always a possibility, with a crossing like that. A
random shot in the torchlight, although the range and
accuracy of a revolver — a hand-held revolver — would
have argued against it. The Vopos are very thorough in their
training. We get details of things like that. The techniques are
to be admired, from a professional point of view. They are
rehearsed in several contingency plans. Such a shame
Echtmann told the girl so little. If he had told her more —
even a little more — or if she had been more intelligent

herself, she would have been just as valuable as he." He looked directly at Clark. "Did Gorlish offer you tea?" Clark nodded. "I thought so. And you refused?" A second nod, a confirming inclination of the head. "Yes, I thought that, too."

The Dane stood up without warning. "I selected you to handle the crossing. You were my choice, major. One day, perhaps, I will tell you why. Incidentally, the East German government are very upset. They have put out an hysterical statement this morning, through the ADN press agency in East Berlin. The irony escapes them, or they ignore it. They shoot their own people, even children, as all the world knows perfectly well. I am not concerned about that. One can make our politicians make the right noises, apologetic or indignant as the case demands. Shall we look at the map room?"

It was some distance away; again of stone blocks and distemper; a wide room, with telephonists — men and women — seated at desks on the left and, to the right, a map of Europe, encompassing the southern, ragged fringes of Ireland to the west, Moscow to the east and parts of the Urals; a relief map with the mountains shaded mauve and their summits white, the lowlands differing degrees of green, indicating altitude. Two men on wooden ladders placed adhesive symbols on it by hand.

Clark and the Dane were by the door, observers not anxious to intrude.

"You know something of it already," the Dane said. "The major nuclear installations are not, of course, involved in the movement. One does not transfer weapons with a range of 10,000 kilometres. There is no need. They are on standby at this moment — which I interpret as full alert — in Russia itself, in East Germany, in the forward bases; in Czechoslovakia and in Hungary. There is no direct confirmation from Poland. We will have that within a few days."

"But the tanks . . . ?"

"The conventional armies are being brought up. Echtmann had observed this very clearly; even the girl had. So have many others. We have varied sources. The short range weapons are being brought up, too. They may carry nuclear warheads, they may not. This, too, is unconfirmed. If only one could borrow a warhead, and have the specialists look at it. . . ."

The two men on the ladders moved constantly at the bidding of the telephonists who called out map-references; the symbols were adjusted or new ones were added.

The Dane touched Clark's arm, signifying that they should go. When they were back in the corridor, he said: "If we were not soldiers, you and I, I could make you a proposition. Since we are soldiers, I cannot. The British Army of the Rhine have been very sympathetic. They have put you at my disposal." Clark stood, the heavy coat encompassing him like a curtain. "If we want you. Perhaps we shall." The Royal *we,* the implication of the infallible hierarchy. "We must descend now. It is not very far. It would be better to walk."

Clark thought of his daughter. He looked at his watch. Almost five. Subtract an hour for the time difference; almost four. She'd have finished school for the day and be coming down Unthank Road, past the factory gates of Derby, in her uniform. Fifteen. An old fifteen. Where had the years gone? She had slender white legs and a slight body. She would have some homework tonight, which she would do while watching television, text book on her lap.

They were walking towards a stairway next to the lift, the Dane ahead.

Fifteen, Clark kept thinking. Fifteen. The breasts had only begun to form. Protrusions beneath the tunic. But fifteen: Old enough to rape. . . .

The stairs followed the lift shaft; ten steps down, turn left, ten steps down, turn left, ten steps down. . . .

"If it comforts you," the Dane said, "the grass will grow

on the bombsites and the children will play with rag balls among the broken masonry The wind will disperse the fallout, if there is a fallout, up to Antartica or wherever. The air will be cleansed. Men will scrabble amongst the masonry, will drag it onto heaps, and will begin to rebuild; will make love so that the the women will bear the children who will play with rag balls." He walked quickly and precisely, sure of his step in the shadowy light. "The children will read in their history books and regard, properly, what has happened as history. Another shifting European alliance, another war, as remote as the others; another bleeding; just as it has always been. The victors are the victors who must lose because they wish to impose themselves rigidly, and the currents will change again in ways they have not forseen. It is only special to us because it is our turn and we cannot look beyond the winning and the losing. Later on, the children will see us, correctly, as creatures in a museum; wax-works to be placed, if we are lucky, alongside Louis Quatorze and Napoleon and Ney and Bismark and Wellington and Montgomery and some of the Russian Czars. Excuse me if I do not place them in chronological order."

They reached the bottom of the stairs. Another corridor faithfully reproducing the lay-out of the floors above; a door at the end, ajar.

"There are Russian advisers in France now. The French were never in NATO anyway. Excuse me if I state the obvious." Clark was unsure quite what the Dane was talking about.

"There is no hard evidence of direct involvement there, yet. Just people in raincoats with anonymous faces: Technical advisers, the umbrella term for everything. But they've turned the French army. And here we are in the middle." They were at the door; they remained outside, out of ear-shot, until the Dane had finished speaking. "The bludgeon from the east, the stab in the back from the west. In tactical parlance, one cannot be happy with this. There are Russian advisers in Italy, too, particularly in the Alpine regions. I am told it is almost impossible to get across the Brenner Pass. The autobahn has been severed, and all traffic, even normal, commercial traffic, is simply turned back. That was two days ago."

"I don't understand. . . ."

"I know you do not, major. I am telling you this because I have picked you and now you must appreciate the urgency of . . . of what you must do." They were very close, and their eyes met. The Dane reached out his hand and gripped Clark's arm, tightening the long fingers around it in a tourniquet. "I do not want your English sensibilities to inhibit you,"

"I was in Korea."

"I am acquainted with that. It is in your record, the places and the dates. The skeleton of a human being, dried and preserved in official jargon. A wireless operator. Not required to do more than receive and transmit. And watch the others fight. I know about the medals, too. I discount medals, major, as a matter of principle. They are given to active soldiers as a reward. They have the worth of bus tickets. Shall we go in?"

The Dane released his arm suddenly.

It was a circular room, stone floor, stone walls, naked and undecorated, just bare blocks cemented together; and yellow lights, like torches, set into the stonework at intervals, above head high; a room for an inquisition, lacking only the metal hoops to secure the wrists to the wall and the wooden frame to stretch the body across; an unfurnished room, except for the table in the middle of it, beyond the reach of the wall-lights and mostly in shadow, with two men already seated behind it. The third chair, the empty chair, was for the Dane. Clark was to stand. Three old faces, watching him; was it their age, or the shadow they were in, or just them? Clark wasn't sure. They sat in silence, predators. Six hands on the table, lain, unmoving, there; and nothing else, no tape recorder, no pencil, no blotting pad, no ash tray, no notebook; nothing except the varnished surface of the table and, before the man who sat in the middle, a buff folder, secured with white ribbon.

"You may stand at ease," the Dane said, his voice altered, remote and official. "At ease, not easy."

Clark was ten feet from the table. He moved his stance to the correct position, hands behind his back.

The man in the middle was English, the other American. The Englishman undid the knot in the ribbon and opened the folder, shuffled some sheaves of paper, arranged them fastidiously. "John Andrew Clark," the Englishman read, the dull, monotone of the lesson in church, pitched forward at nobody and anybody. "Born Ware, Hertfordshire, the second of the fifth, 1932. Father John Paul Clark. Died the twenty first of the seventh, 1955." The voice altered, as the Dane's had done. "The cause of death is not noted. How very bad. Mother still living. Educated, Bishop's Stortford Grammar School, matriculated . . ." But Clark wasn't listening now. He knew the particulars better than they. Of course. It was his life . . .

"Joined the British Army at Pirbright, the fifth of the fifth, 1949 as a trainee wireless operator. Forty third Hussars. Active service in Korea, embarking the second of the tenth . . ."

The American shifted his position on his chair and folded his arms. He must have been bored, too. He wore a slate-grey, light uniform with two rows of ribbons and medals. Clark remembered what the Dane had said: Bus tickets. Clark looked at the Dane, who had settled like an old bird on its nest and was now at peace, staring at the darkened ceiling. There was no touch of vanity pinned to his uniform, no portable credential; he didn't need it.

"Military intelligence . . ." The Englishman's voice bored onward, measured and precise. "Mombasa, Kenya . . .

seconded to the Royal Navy." He coughed to clear his throat. The diction must not be impaired. "The reports say that your work was satisfactory. I assume the selection of that word implies competence and little else. It is curious. Perhaps you, too, will agree on this, major: The word recurs in the reports of your work in the Federal Republic of Germany. Satisfactory. After more than two decades, major, one is entitled to hope that you are, at the very least, satisfactory. If you were not, one would be entitled — compelled — to wonder just what you had been doing."

Clark nodded his head stupidly.

He wanted to say something just then, to stop this dried chronicling of the dates in his life and say what had been troubling him so deeply for a week, ten days maybe: A fear of the retreat. He had contemplated it, as if it were inevitable. They were better armed, better trained; they were more numerous in everything, ships, rockets, troops, transport, submarines, tanks . . .

The retreat. He'd seen one before, in Korea, although reality like that never strayed into official folders. The gunfire from over the hill, the garbled instructions, the shifting command post, always keeping ahead of the tide of battle, mobile and on the move, now camped at a cross-roads, now in a deserted village; and the wounded in the hedge-rows, and no-one to tend them. The days unshaven, unkempt, knowing that your own effort, however great, could alter nothing; the nights, lit by the gunfire which threaded across the sky and died as quickly as a cheap children's firework.

He'd wondered what it would be like this time, the retreat. They'd be going back to the west, because the German villages would have been replaced by Dutch villages; and then Flemish; and they would be close when the gulls were in the fields, undisturbed by the gunfire. And the nights would be spent with an ear cupped against a radio set, listening to the helpless commands and, maybe, the BBC World Service news bulletins with women, no doubt, reading the bulletins, short, rational evaluations suggesting that all was going well. The refugees would be on the road again, just as before, the women shepherding the children, pushing wheel-barrows and handcarts loaded with what they had salvaged; and, behind them, the very old, abandoned because the mothers had to press on with the children — the primeval, preservative instinct — westward, struggling to keep in front of the gunfire, the worn-out shoes and the bleeding, blistered feet and the crying of the children, lost; the low planes coming in over the trees, raking them thoughtlessly, friend or foe, soldier or civilian, adult or child, all indistinguishable to the pilot behind the goggles in a cockpit, high and safe, with only a single button to stroke to make the column of stragglers break up and fall and die. Mistakes will not be punished. The sand dunes and the sea. There is no shelter, not in Ostend, not in Rotterdam, not in Zebrugge; not this time. The last of the boats has already gone. Dunkirk is unavailable, by order of the French government. You stay. You lie there, with the exhausted children under your skirts and sand in your finger nails, and cry if you want. Nobody will listen. The tanks are coming. Perhaps you can hear them already, the iron tread biting into the tarmacadam. There will be a bureau for displaced persons, soon, run by the comrades. They'll have a plan. You'll see. No redress, if you don't like the plan. Churchill is dead, these fifteen years. Maybe we can't do it again. Maybe we don't want it another time. You'll find out.

"The case of Echtmann — or incident, or error — is curious." The Englishman talked on. "When he ran towards the wire, he ran directly to it. It is in your report. He made no attempt to zig-zag, to make himself a more difficult target. What can he have been thinking of?" Another cough. "Unless he was not told what to do. Did you tell him, major?"

Clark said; "I did not think it was necessary . . ."

". . . and if you had not been wrong about this, Echtmann might have been here with us. All the arrangements were entrusted to you. Two decades. One might have expected competence, at least in the basics."

Echtmann was 22; not exactly a child. What was Clark supposed to do: Vault the wire himself and hold his hand?

"You have had an ordinary career. That is my word. Limited responsibility, discharged with a minimum of originality, even when that was obviously required. One may place little or no store upon people who spent, as you did, major, two years in the waterfront bars of Mombasa, crudely eavesdropping on the local gossip and returning to Royal naval bases to say that it was all the gospel truth . . ."

Somewhere out of sight, a fan turned with a purring noise; the rhythm of a humming bird, endlessly beating its wings.

"Echtmann: Was he not briefed, told the exact distance he had to cover, advised in the greatest detail exactly how to do it?" A third cough, held in the upper throat and mouth, a nervous affectation, not a malady. "Clearly he was not. Most clearly he was not. You had to order a soldier to kill him. At least you included that in your report. How touching. But you cannot absolve yourself by writing it down, major. The error remains."

Clark knew perfectly well that, if this was some kind of trial — and the two decades had taught him this — it was not yet the moment to defend himself. That might come later; it might not. At the moment, he was being asked questions and forbidden from answering them.

He felt hot. The air-conditioning had dried the atmosphere, and he felt slight pain in his lungs at each inhalation.

The American produced a photograph from his pocket, held it out and motioned for Clark to come forward and examine it. It was the size of a postcard, and in black and white: A missile on the back of a lorry, its cone tilted upward and reaching beyond the driver's cabin.

"An S 33," Clark said, assuming that that was what was expected of him. He replaced it on the table, in front of the American.

"You were told to hold it. You were not told to return it." The Dane had opened his eyes and spoke quickly. Clark, drawn between picking it up again or leaving it alone, did nothing. He resumed his stance: Soldier's obedience.

"How did you know what it was?" The American had a New England accent, soft and civilised.

"Because I recognised it." Clark permitted himself the little sarcasm. It was the only way he could defend himself.

The Englishman said: "I was expecting many things from you. I was not expecting the juvenile. Your conduct here is consistent with your record."

And Clark wanted to say: You brought me here, you set up Echtmann's crossing and ordered me to do it; you wanted me, I didn't want you; and now this. The hostility I can take. I'm an old dog now, and all that nonsense doesn't matter a damn. I was in Korea. I saw the killing, the guts on the baked roads. And it's all going to happen here. It was the Chinese then, the Russians now. The difference is academic. Where will you be then, you clever bastards? Gone on the Sabena flight with friend Gorlish, back to Whitehall and crouching in a bomb shelter, eating decontaminated tinned food?

"I was in Korea, too," the Englishman said, as if he had sensed all this with great clarity. "And not as a wireless operator."

A moment of silence.

"The S 33," the American observed. "It could have been another marque . . ."

"On the 31 and 32, the fins are significantly longer and flatter."

"How many fins?"

"On the 33, six at each side, in a cluster."

"And the 32?"

"Four each side."

"And the 31?"

"Also four at each side."

Another photograph, the same size but with an inkless embossed stamp in the bottom right hand corner: Property of NATO. A soldier, standing alone, smoking. It must have been taken at a railway station. The lip of the platform could be seen, and a section of rail.

"Which regiment?" The American again, the technical expert.

"Byelorussian. I don't know which regiment. Only the army group."

"Why not?" It was the Englishman now, interpreting the answers. "What if it was important to recognise it? What if you saw it briefly at a railway station — through the window of a passing train — and then it was gone?"

Come on, Joanne. How is the homework tonight? I hope you ate a good meal, plenty of meat and potatoes. Please don't watch television so much, it will damage your eyes. . .

Clark had begun to sweat. He could feel the moisture rising on his forehead, in the shallow creases of the skin, and a dropletor two flowing down into his eyebrows, irritating him terribly. Still his hands were locked behind his back. "I do not speak," the Englishman said pointedly, "of the loose gossip in the bars of Mombasa. I speak of the elementary aspects of what you should be able to do: Recognise, identify, codify . . ."

"There are three Byelorussian army groups . . ." Clark began.

"Everybody knows that," the American said. "Probably even the cleaning women here know that. Three army groups. Half a million men, and you cannot make the difference."

Clark did not reply.

"We are waiting, major," the Englishman said.

The sweat was in his armpits and the small of his back.

The eyes across the table seemed so cool, as if they were not subject to the dried air.

"Nobody can recognise them all," Clark said at length. He had been ordered to defend himself now. "There are East Germans, Poles, Hungarians, Czechs, Rumanians, Bulgarians, all the Russians. And now the French, too."

Silence again, the communal silence of conspirators; the silence to mark his own inadequacy. The registering of it with no comment; the condemnation of himself by his own words — the kind the bureaucrats love best of all . . .

"But you are employed to recognise them all." Was it that they were both English which allowed the Englishman to be like this? Clark looked away. "You will look at me." And then, "You were told to stand at ease. In that position your eyes should be directly ahead. A novice cadet could tell you that."

The Dane said: "What were the circumstances of your divorce?"

"I won't discuss that."

"I could put you on a charge for a statement like that," the Englishman said.

"Try it."

"It is said your wife was unfaithful," the Dane continued. "That she went with another man; a private in the British Army of the Rhine. When did she first make love to him?"

Have you finished the homework, Joanne? Yes, I know you are fifteen now but because I am much older, I know you think you are already an adult when you are not. I expect you have a boyfriend. I wish I had met him. I remember that you used to ask why daddy doesn't come home any more. I heard you one night, when I was in the hall and you didn't know. The lounge door was open, and that was how I heard. I'd brought you a present. I can't remember what the occasion was. But when I heard that, I just went away. I expect

Mummy gave you the present and pretended she had bought it . . .

Clark's hands were almost clenched, skin against skin, the release of pressure on the self. The sweat was flowing freely, and it must have showed.

"He wasn't a private," Clark said. "He was a lance corporal. They did it in a Volkswagen in a carpark outside Hannover, after eating an Indonesian meal. He wasn't very competent and she thought she was going to have an attack of cramp. Excuse me if I don't recognise the fins on the car, and which side they were. Anything else?"

"But you've a daughter," the Dane said. "Have you provided for her properly? Does she have the right clothes for school? And how do you ensure this, when you are stationed in Germany and your wife and daughter are in the midlands of England?"

"Go to hell," Clark said evenly. "You go to hell. And take the other two ponces with you. It's hotting up. The tanks are coming. Time for you to run away."

The American pushed back his chair. "If that was a test," he said, "thank Christ he passed."

TUESDAY

Cologne at four in the afternoon, and the rain falling on the grey Rhine. Clark stood by the railings, alone, his coat collar turned up, surveying the undulating expanse of water. Below the parapet, the water lapped against concrete blocks, and a film of green kitchen indicated high water mark. In the distance, under the span of the metal railway bridge, a tug burrowed upstream, towing a barge draped in tarpaulin. Behind Clark, a thin strip of scenic stones, mixed pink and blue, and broken every thirty yards by leafless trees; and, behind that, the dual carriageway, heavy with cars. He could hear the thin scraping of windscreen wipers as the cars edged slowly by, up to the traffic lights.

We've picked you to be the guardian. Or the custodian, if you prefer. Klaus is the brilliant one. A degree, you know, when he was only twenty-one. He's twenty eight now, by the way.

The tug drew abreast and Clark could see somebody in a blue, peaked cap down in the cabin, navigating it.

We want a man found, the Dane had said. They were back in his office. Clark had anticipated an apology, or at least, a smoothing, after the insults. He had got nothing, just a briefing. You will wonder why we want one particular man found. I will tell you: He has stolen some papers and run away with them. They are very important papers. He wants to sell them, to us or in the east. He has put out his feelers in both places. Echtmann knew of the feeler in the east. That is why we had to try to get him across the wire. The girl, of course, knew nothing of this. Klaus knows the name of the man who stole the papers. Klaus will find him. You'll see.

The tug had gone, and now Clark gazed across the river to the park on the far bank.

You're to go with Klaus. Everywhere. If he goes to the toilet, you wait directly outside the door for him. You make sure Klaus doesn't do anything . . . anything extravagant. He's so young. Before the War, they would have prized him. The Teutonic strain is very strong in him. Incidentally, I have some American travellers cheques for you. They are made out in your name. You can cash them anywhere, as they are needed. Your own name seemed perfectly secure. After all, nobody has heard of you.

Clark heard the chimes from the cathedral, a colossal edifice rising above the buildings up the incline towards the town; the spires ornate and reaching up into the leaden sky like spread fingers. He turned and faced it, waiting until each of the four heavy thuds had echoed and died away. Exactly four o'clock.

The car is in your name, too. I'm sorry, it's only a Rekord. I have the insurance certificate here, a general cover. The police will accept this, in case of accidents.

Clark wandered along to the traffic lights and crossed.

I must ask you some questions, Clark had said. What exactly has this man stolen? And what is his name? And how much time have we? The Dane's voice was measured. What he stole is no concern of yours. Klaus knows, and that is enough. His name is Arthur Dahlem, and he is a German citizen. Klaus has the personal details: Age, height, medical report, shoe-size, this manner of information. Also some photographs. Time? I can give you a few days. Perhaps a week.

On the other side, Clark turned along the row of warehouses which flanked the dual carriageway; one closed down, another with a loading platform high up, and a pulley, rocking gently in the wind. Clausings was marked by a red neon sign secured to the wall above the door and, beneath it, in smaller letters — in white, on a black background — pulsating on and off: Adult Films. A lime green curtain had been drawn discreetly across the wide window, revealing nothing of the interior. The door was of polished wood and two columns of studs, equidistant, had been driven into it.

Another question. Just one more, sir. May I call you sir? I'm more comfortable like that. It seems more natural and more correct. The Dane had nodded, as if it were a great indulgence to grant this last question. The Dane's mood had changed. He wanted this over, he wanted to get on with other things. Clark asked: Will there be another war? I've a daughter, you see. Of course, you know that. You questioned me about it. But she is my daughter. The Dane said nothing. Then he said: You have seen the operations room for yourself. Echtmann could have told us a great deal. That is why I selected you, major, as the man to ensure he would make the crossing. If there is guilt, perhaps we will share it. He smiled, a watery smile, contrived for this moment and charged with insincerity.

Clark grasped the heavy brass handle and opened the door. Inside, he had to step through a curtain to get into the room. It was almost all in shadow, a tasteless room, decorated on the cheap: A crude covering of floorboards running away to the bar in one corner with glass shelves up the wall behind it and bottles on them, some upturned and their necks held in chromium clenches, to dispense exact measures; a waitress leaned forward across the bar counter. She wore a black, sequined dress, cut away at the front to allow her breasts to hang naked and free. Blue veins were weaved beneath the skin. Clark thought distantly of the Dane's hands, on the desk. He surveyed the room. Two more girls sat on stools at the end of the bar, drinking coffee from plastic beakers. They must have had to send out for them, unless there was a kettle secreted under the counter. Around the other walls, semi-circular seats were arranged with tables in front of them. A small man, encased in a raincoat he had not unbuttoned, sat in one, adjusting his spectacles. He had a single bottle of beer in front of him and an empty glass. Perhaps he didn't drink. He'd come for the film show.

Klaus was at the back, much further away. He lifted a hand to signify recognition. The girls had watched Clark. Now they turned back and talked between themselves. Clark walked over.

Twenty-eight. Klaus looked just that. He was unconsciously confident, the confidence of physical strength and youth. His face had been blemished by a skin disorder in childhood or, more likely, in adolescence; extinct craters lay across it, as if shrapnel had burst across him, long ago.

Clark stood a couple of yards away. His hair was wet from the rain, and he pressed it down with the palm of his hand.

Klaus: Sharply-defined, even in the shadow. His hair was long, though short of the Biblical length; it was full, concealing the ears completely. Specks of dried skin lay in a descending crescent around his shoulders, and must have fallen from the scalp. The flying jacket he wore had been cut — or torn — on the left side, and sown with thick, secure thread. Clark looked squarely at him, sitting there: The hair was blond.

The madame, a heavy woman in a red dress which clung to her, was standing uneasily on a wooden chair, struggling with the projector which stood on a shelf and pointed towards the screen, hanging on a wall near the bar; her thick fingers pressed against the controls, manipulating them to no effect.

Clark sat down opposite Klaus.

"There is only one price," Klaus said. "It's ten marks, whatever you want to drink."

Clark nodded.

One of the girls appeared. She wore too much lipstick. Clark regarded her exposed breasts clinically, as one might survey the headlines of a newspaper someone else is reading. They were petite, to be polite. Here, that hardly mattered. It was only biological curiosity.

"I want a beer," Clark said. "Any kind . . ."

Klaus said: "I'll have a coffee . . ."

"We don't serve coffee here." She was prim and proper, like an air hostess: You must look at me, you must admire my chic, but God help you if you reach out a hand to touch. . . .

"But you're drinking it." Klaus was impatient and drifting towards aggression.

She shugged, and that made her breasts oscillate briefly. "Get me one."

The girl called to the madame. "He wants a coffee."

The madame, still poised on the chair — the high-heels she wore were making it like a circus act, and might have given way at any moment — bristled. A battle-axe, fifty-five and no shocks left for her. Her hair had been permed and lay like coils of barbed wire about her head. "If you want coffee, you can get out of here." She was partially out of breath from the stretching.

"Then tell your employees not to drink it." Klaus was upset; or feigning it. He turned to the girl. 'I'll have a glass of water. With ice. Plenty of ice. At least five cubes."

"It will cost you ten marks."

"I can read the notice on the wall. Don't you think I can read?" His eyes were livid with anger.

Just then, the screen sprang to life, out of focus and with the picture off-centre, so that the bottom right-hand corner was missing altogether. The title had already passed, lost in the technical difficulties. The action had begun, A pallid couple copulated mechanically in what appeared to be an hotel room; there was no warmth in the decor, no personal memento, no family photograph, no worn-down carpet slippers. A pallid couple, moving from position to position, as if to demonstrate their repertoire.

It was very curious, Clark thought, how they never kissed, never touched each other, never embraced for the pleasure of an embrace, but continued, the pivots and fulcrums and pistons of the human anatomy, employed, in public, for financial gain.

The madame was calling back to the barmaid, loudly, and absolutely insensitive as to whether the volume of her voice was destroying the pleasure of the film for the customers; she wanted to know if it was in focus.

Clark looked at Klaus again: The soiled, full lining of the flying jacket protruded; a ruffled shirt in a tartan pattern; and jeans, and brown, mountain-climbing boots, the rubber soles rutted for grip.

"The films are rubbish," Klaus said. "They make them all up in Hamburg, the same people doing the same things." He lifted his arm again, gesticulating vaguely towards the screen. "The man has a birthmark on his backside." Clark, as he was bidden, scanned the screen; saw the man's thin legs, flecked with dark hairs, rise and fall. "It's not a trick," Klaus said. He was very earnest, as if this was important. "They're really doing it. You will see in just a moment. He will ejaculate openly, in order to prove he has had a climax."

The man in the raincoat was watching captivated, his beer forgotten.

The madame stepped heavily down from the chair, grunted, and walked towards the bar. Reinforcements, Clark thought. The barmaid with big breasts, and the madame with a big body. He nearly smiled.

The waitress returned, holding Clark's beer in one hand, the glass over the neck of the bottle; the glass of water in the other, the ice cubes beating noisily against the side of the glass, like a swilling tide. "Twenty marks," she said. She had her purse out, ready to accept the money, to offer the change. They hesitated, unsure who was going to pay. Clark took out a twenty-mark note.

"And for service. . . .?"

"Nothing," Klaus said, intervening heavily. "You don't give her one damned pfennig."

But Clark did give her a two mark piece.

The film ended and another began without warning; began with a series of numbers working downward, in a countdown, to one, zero; then, in colour, the legend: A Swedish production. Just that. No names named; no producer, no director, no costume consultant, no cast list; no title, even, as if that would have been both irrelevant and presumptious. Colour, uncertain, ill-defined colour, but a degree better than black and white. Three couples, partly sun-tanned — but revealing the marks of the bathing costumes, interlocked in improbable combinations upon a sofa.

Klaus drank of the water, wiped his mouth with the sleeve of the flying jacket. Clark had left his beer where it had been placed, the glass still over the neck of the bottle. "They put some pressure on you," Klaus said. "They told me that. You might not like me. It's been known." He shifted the glass of water across the table-top to another place, sliding it, its base never leaving the surface. The ice clicked, lump against lump, bobbing up and down. "Maybe it's the best thing," he said. "Some more slaughter, some more blood-letting. People were bled, in olden times, to make them get better."

"Generally they died."

Klaus ignored that. He wanted a monologue, a lecture; not a discussion. "Maybe the Russians should come. They're spiritualists. They know that eggs come from chickens behind the house, and you have to feed the chickens properly. . . ." He drank, letting the ice buffet against his face, then slip back into the glass. "The Americans will run away again. They'll term that isolationism, they'll convince themselves of their own rationale. Or whatever. They won't press the button. Too bad." His eyes drifted back towards the screen. The pairings had altered. One girl was being abused unmercifully; she was upside down, her lean legs clipped over the back of the sofa; her hair in a pool about her head.

The Dane had said: Klaus may be difficult. Handle him gently. He's a failure, in spite of the degree. Four years at univerisity, being feted. Then nothing. He couldn't even hold down a proper job. Until we found him. He's alright, underneath. Twenty-eight. Very young. Coming to everything for the first time. He's a professional cynic. He jeers at everything — the terrible 1960's emptiness which he will masquerade as truth if you let him. He wants to work for us, in spite of the intellectual arguments and contradictions. He always been like that, right from the beginning. Don't join the arguments; allow him to convince himself. He'll do that, right enough.

"The Russians will destroy all this, if they come," Klaus said. "The whole Common Market nonsense, paid for by us — by the Germans. The exodus from Brussels should be worth seeing." He summoned one of the girls, indicating that he wanted the one who had not served them. The madame was on the telephone, explaining to somebody how many customers they had. Seven, she lied. The girl came, tall, dark haired.

"I only sit down with you if you buy champagne," she said. She sounded vaguely offended when he shook his head. "Don't you know how to entertain a lady?"

"A beer for her," Klaus called out.

She sat next to Klaus, strategically placing herself neither too close nor too distant; to be touched, perhaps, but not mauled. His left hand reached over and searched for her exposed breast, his eyes remaining directly towards Clark; found it, investigated its circumference with his fingers, and stroked it mechanically. The girl was watching Clark, too, but, most oddly, he didn't feel like a voyeur at all. Clark wondered only how she could control the nerve-tissues, being fondled in public and showing perfect indifference, by anybody who had the price of a beer.

"You know something," Klaus said. The girl had thrown her head back and closed her eyes as his fingers tightened around the nipple. "A lot of people want another war. They think we'll win this one. They think the Russians will roll over us, and then they'll get weak. And when they get weak, they'll start to change. They'll look at our autobahns, our houses, our clothes and say to themselves: Hey, wait a minute, comrade, what's so wrong with this capitalism?" His hand drifted up to the girl's shoulder and moved down her back, to the zip of her dress. "Maybe the people who think that are wrong. It's only an idea."

"And what do you think?" Clark asked.

"I'll screw the girl first, and wonder about that afterwards." She had begun to protest and tried, limply, to push his arm away, but he had pressed her forward, the zip was down to her buttocks, and the dress fallen completely away at the front.

The man in the raincoat was terribly drawn between watching the film or watching Klaus, out of the corner of his eye. The madame was appraising the situation; she'd have been happier if he had bought the champagne: Then he could have taken the girl, there and then, on the floorboards. She held up a bottle. A cheap blue label. "Fifty marks," she called out.

But Klaus leant away from the girl, drank a little water, and laughed and laughed and laughed.

Clark wandered up to the cathedral, the wind plucking fitfully at his overcoat. A group of schoolchildren stood in a crocodile at the main door, waiting to go in. They were very small and held hands, regardless of the sex of the partner. Some of the children were black, and Clark thought it couldn't be a German party; English or French, probably. Then he remembered. The French weren't travelling abroad any more, not since the vote.

He walked across the cathedral square towards a cafe. The rush hour had begun, and a grey, restless tide of office workers — as drained as the waters of the Rhine, down there, down the hill — moved from the new shopping precinct across the square to the ranks of stone steps, descending, flowing across the road and entering the railway station.

Five twenty. Two hours to kill. Klaus would have finished with the girl by then.

Clark saw the newspaper poster in the distance, outside a shop in the precinct; saw the word Belgian and a second word, in equally large type, beneath it; strained to read it: Crisis. The wind caught the poster and twisted it, held it half-folded over, released it.

And still the office workers came, passing the poster as if it did not exist. Only the newspaper shop remained open; and a pornographic bookshop, further down, its window full of Doctor somebody's lotions, and grotesque sexual aids, and some magazines of both men and women; but their genitals had been discreetly covered by while circles of adhesive labels which, doubtless, the proprietor had placed there. Clark bought a paper. The headlines were spread fully across the front page: Belgium neutral!

He walked back towards the cathedral, lost among the workers, borne forward by them. The cathedral loomed, monstrous, in the ebbing, failing light and the sky was full of running cloud, black and satanic. Ten to five. The Rekord wasn't far away; in the underground carpark. The American Forces Network news bulletin was on the hour. He was there in time; turned the volume control full up, because the concrete overhead robbed the radio signals of their strength.

Five. A zylaphone, being played in an ascending scale, the jingle to precede the bulletin. Then a woman's voice. "This is Frankfurt. News on the hour, every hour, from the wires of AP and UPI" She paused, the incantation ended, and the pause to indicate this. "The government of Belgium met in emergency session last night. The session finished midnight, central European time.

"Prime Minister Pierre Leclerc made this statement to reporters." A recording, of a voice with a French accent, muffled and uncertain as it coped with the hand-held microphones. "The government of the Kingdom of Belgium have decided to recommend to King Leopold that the nation withdraws immediately from all existing military treaties, commitments and obligations."

It was true. They'd gone neutral. Clark breathed heavily.

A reporter's voice: "Does that include NATO?"

"Obviously." The question seemed to offend the Prime Minister. "When the royal assent is obtained, we shall apply to the United Nations in New York to have our decision formally recognised, and we shall have it recorded with the Geneva Convention."

"What about the Common Market?"

"We see no reason why we should not remain members. Italy is still a member, and we greatly regret that the French decided to leave after their general election. That is all, gentlemen. A full statement will be available tomorrow, from the parliamentary press office. Good night."

Now another voice, an American, assessing it: "The Belgian decision comes at a time of acute tension in Europe. Presumably, Belgian combat troops will be withdrawn from their positions in the Federal Republic. The Belgian contribution is small — around 15,000 men — and statements from NATO headquarters this morning indicate the gaps will be covered from existing reservists. However,

Prime Minister Leclerc did indicate that the NATO headquarters itself, now located on Belgian soil, would have to be transferred elsewhere since, as he put it, its presence infringes Belgian neutrality. Informed sources late today say the transfer is expected to be carried out within two or three days."

Clark closed his eyes in the contemplation of it: The loading of tons of paper onto lorries, the convoys down the autoroute to Aachen and across into the Federal Republic, the absolute administrative chaos; the telephone installations, the coding machines, the secretaries, the things lost in transit . . . the nerve centre spread out. Dear God. What if the tanks moved then?

He wondered about Gorlish; and about the Dane.

The radio was still on. "In other news, floods have reportedly claimed seven lives in Michigan, South Korean president appeals to the US Congress for more strike planes, and the Australian couple who are marrying each other for the third time. After this announcement."

A man's voice, patronising enough to be almost sickly: "America was founded on a Declaration that all men are equal, no matter what colour their skin, no matter what their creed or religion. So, servicemen, if you have any problems, go right along to your social habilitation officer. You'll find the nearest office in your camp directory. . . ."

Clark turned it off. He walked slowly back to the square and found a restaurant; ate some sausages and saurkraut, using the mustard liberally. He drank a couple of big beers and wondered if he ought to ring Brussels, to get the new telephone number in the Federal Republic, for when the transfer was complete. He did nothing.

Six thirty. He decided to go and get Klaus. Too bad if he was early.

An old house in Berliner Strasse, with a small, abandoned

garden in front of it. The rain had begun again. Clark parked outside, walked along the crazy-paving. The door wasn't locked. Three floors up, mounting bare, uncovered stairs, he found the apartment. Number 7B. He knocked, heard muted, muffled sound from within and Klaus came, knotting the cloth belt of a tartan dressing gown. "You're early," he said. It was an attic — or, more precisely, what an optimistic French estate agent would have described as a studio.

The angle of the roof enabled a grown man to stand upright only to one side of it; to gain the bed required a crouch. The girl was in the bed, the sheets drawn protectively over her.

The kitchenette had been constructed in a corner, of simple hardboard partitions tacked to a wooden frame. Klaus stood on the linoleum in bare feet, putting the kettle on.

Clark looked at the girl.

"What is this?" the girl called out, in German.

"A man," Klaus replied, taunting her. "He wants to see your body. Rip the sheets off and show him. He'll give you five marks, if you're lucky." And then, to Clark: "Tea or coffee?"

"Whatever you're making."

"Don't worry about the girl. A whore. She's supposed to be at a teacher's training college. She only works in Clausing's twice a week. I had to wait. She doesn't finish until five thirty. They treat them like office workers. . . ." He came out of the kitchen. The kettle had been filled and switched on. "I'll show you what kind of a whore she is." He went to the bed, opened her fingers so that she released the sheet, and pulled it off the bed. As she began to rise, naked, he pressed her back down. "The visitor wants an exhibition. He wants to see some action." She swore at him. "The student teacher gets real lessons here. Hey, she likes an audience. She really does." Again she swore. Klaus drew her from the bed and made her face Clark. He was behind her, holding her hands.

She twisted her head to one side in shame. "Feel her," Klaus said. "Everybody else does. Those dock workers on the quay side, they go to Clausing's at lunch time with their dirty hands and play with her. She likes that."

She swore again.

"Tell her to get out," Clark said.

Klaus released her and she went away into a corner to dress. Klaus went back to the kitchen, unplugged the kettle. "Don't come back tonight," he said to the girl. "Don't come back any night." When she had gone, he said: "I went to university. They tell you that? I got a degree. I'm a real live doctor of philosophy. It was well worth it." With a sweep of his arm, he took in the unmade bed, the lace curtains only half covering the single window; the little television set on a small side-table, with some beer bottles alongside it and, further away, a white plate, a knife and fork abandoned on it and some reddish sauce congealed at its rim. "I gave them four years of my life for this." Paperback books were stored in a tea chest against one wall. "There was a TV programme last night. A special programme, about the villages near the frontier. If you own a car, load it and get out. That was the message. They interviewed people. Know what one old woman said: The Russians can't take my pension away, can they?" He laughed, a strange, insincere laugh. "You know what NATO is? A few long-haired teenagers, a few stupid people who couldn't find any other job, a few British and a few Americans. In the east, it's not like that. They've got women working on the roads with drills, carrying stone blocks by hand. The women over there would handle the Bundeswehr. Prosit — cheers, to you." They both drank from the mugs.

The professional cynic. The Dane had said that. Clark wanted to say somethng else: Listen, sonny, you were brought up in prosperity, you went to university; you didn't see them, the women and children coming back along the road from Kaesong. You were only two then. You didn't see the procession, struggling away from the cluster of huts with the straw roofs on fire and the smell thick in your nostrils; you didn't hear the machine gun fire, and the refugees lying, faces pressed down, in the sunken rice fields; you didn't see them come back to the mud road and come forward again, the American military vehicles cutting through them regardless. You didn't hear the slap-slap-slap of naked feet on the baked, hot earth; you didn't see the children abandoned on the side of the track, with stomach wounds and little, brown hands holding the guts in.

He looked directly at Klaus. Complaining about the apartment. Of course. Only enough money for a television and a crate or two of beer. Only enough to hire the girl, and make her do whatever he wanted. I weep for you, he should have said; but he lacked the art of intonation, and could never have made the simple statement into an insult, as he would have wished.

Sonny, sonny. You know it all.

But. . . .

You didn't cradle a little head in your arms, the muted eyes beseeching you, as a God, to stop the pain because you were white and you wore a uniform and you would know how to do it; and you had nothing in your battledress pockets except a few dried biscuits; and an 88 radio set on your back.

He thought of Joanne.

He thought of the camp priest, abasing himself before the altar; he heard that man's words, again and again, as if, once spoken, they could never be erased: Please God, not again.

"We've wasted quite enough time," Clark said curtly. "Now you get dressed."

Their eyes met. It was the first test.

"Go carefully," Klaus said. He was standing by the kitchen door, nursing the mug in both hands. "You go carefully."

They took the autobahn south. The weather reports on the radio were for mist along the Rhine and ice on all roads before midnight, so Clark drove quietly. It suited him, a heavy man hunched over the wheel who found, even after all these years, driving on the right unnatural. They were down past Bonn and nearing Koblenz when Clark spoke.

"What did he pick Munich for?"

"Maybe he's got a sense of humour after all," Klaus said. His eyes were closed, his head and shoulder propped against the passenger window; like an animal in repose, the body slack but ready to tense and move at any moment. "Maybe he wants to re-enact 1939 and the sell-out."

"I've been thinking about it," Clark said. "Munich is near Austria and the Austrians are neutral, of course. If something went wrong and he had to run. . . ."

Klaus said nothing; merely opened his eyes, scanned the traffic on the autobahn and went back to sleep.

They stopped after Karlsruhe, when the monstrous neon-decked plain which was the city, and the rim of suburbs which spread like tentacles into the night, had gone. A raststop. Clark drew into the wide car-park behind the cafeteria. The covered petrol station flanked the autobahn; further away, the heavy lorries rested in their own area, elephantine in the shadows. An old, pale-blue Czech vehicle had lilac curtains drawn round the driver's cab. They went into a wide room lined with varnished wood, the veneer dark and forbidding and pairs of antlers attached, here and there: It had the smell and feel of a bogus hunting lodge. A huge peasant woman in black waitresses' uniform transported meals and drinks on a dented metal tray. A businessman sat at a corner table, absently reading the evening newspaper. Clark saw the headline again: Belgium neutral! Two of the lorry drivers were nearby, sitting facing each other and talking quietly.

Clark went to a table at the window. Klaus sat opposite

him and brushed some crumbs from the white tablecloth. A used cup of coffee lay at his elbow and he moved it away with obvious distaste.

Then he took the photographs from his wallet and laid them in front of Clark, as he might have arranged playing cards, in a line with a certain space between each. Clark looked at them: A slight, serious face masked by plain spectacles which distorted the eyes behind them, enlarging the pupils; and straight, thin, blond hair which lay partially down the forehead.

The traffic from the autobahn made the cafeteria windows vibrate gently and in a constant rhythm, rising and falling.

There were four photographs: Dahlem looking left, right and directly forward; and a profile, taken side-on. He had worn a suit for the occasion — the lapels of it could be seen. He looked serious, an anaemic clerk who might have been poised and preened for an interview with a bank. He had held himself stiff and still for the photographer. It all reminded Clark of a joke he'd heard, years ago: A businessman sat at an enormous desk saying to an employee, "Yes, Smith, you have all the makings of a first-class underling."

He stooped to examine each of the photographs more closely. Each had been stamped in a bottom corner with a serial number; stamped by hand, because the distribution of the ink was uneven, as if the pressure of the stamp had been applied carelessly and the photographs had been only four of a great number of others to be done at one sitting.

"That's what he looked like last April," Klaus said. "They only take them once a year. He could have grown his hair since, or a moustache. Or something."

The waitress came, looking harrassed. "Two coffees," Klaus said, without troubling to look at her, and she went quickly away.

"I asked about his hair, but nobody seemed too sure," Klaus went on. "They didn't notice him, that's the joke. He just sat at his desk year after year. He didn't drink, he didn't smoke, he didn't complain. He didn't try and get the secretaries at the Christmas party. He was always, they said, very correct. I damn nearly laughed in their faces. The bastards. They didn't know one thing about him and they didn't care."

"His file reads like a creature put together by a computer. Under hobbies, he'd written: Visiting my mother. He meant that. Sarcasm was beyond him." The coffee came. The waitress arranged the cups and a jug of milk mechanically, wrote out a small bill, folded it in half, and left it at the end of the table. "He had as much going for him as the tin of paper clips on his desk. Except he was trusted. A little at a time. It took him four years and in the end he was trusted by default. They had no option. He was always there, efficient, secretive, apparently honest. A mole." He drank, but his eyes were on Clark, not the cup. "He started to handle classified material. Why not? And then one day he cleared off. They couldn't believe it. Too damn right they couldn't. They didn't even know he had a driver's licence. He passed the test but he kept that from them, too. It isn't on his file anywhere. Under the question: Can you drive, and give details of experience, he'd just written 'no'." Klaus replaced the cup in the saucer. "Lousy, autobahn coffee," he said bitterly, as if he had been cheated of something important. "They must have dredged it out of a cess-pit."

Clark was still looking at the photographs, although he had not reached out and touched any of them.

Klaus said: "Arthur Dahlem, nonentity, did a little copying here and there. He never disturbed the originals. He never misplaced one single sheet of paper. He just wrote down what he wanted and took it home. He was never even searched. They don't do that kind of thing in Brussels. The British are offended by it — insulting our integrity, they say, some crap like that. So nobody does it. He probably kept what he'd copied in a bank vault somewhere, to make sure it wasn't stolen from him." Klaus bared his teeth in a smile, as if the concept of a man using the system to destroy the system appealed immensely to him.

Clark could hear one of the lorry drivers talking about Berlin, and how he'd been made to wait three and a half hours at Helmstedt to cross the East German frontier. "In Berlin," he said, confidentially, "they're putting up barricades at the street corners. I saw them. The authorities are letting them pull up paving stones and use them. It's like Budapest in 56. It's the same waste of time. The tanks will go straight through them, just push them aside. I offered to bring my grandmother out, let her just sit in the lorry with me. But she wouldn't come. She was crying when I left. She said she wouldn't see me again, but she wanted to die in Berlin. There's a family grave in Spandau. She's already told the priest all about it."

Clark lifted his cup. The coffee was tepid and he drank it all at once, as one takes medicine which is faintly unpleasant.

When they were back in the car, Klaus said: "It will be painless in Berlin. There won't be any fighting. The Americans will get onto their aeroplanes out. West Berlin will go to bed one night good democrats, and wake up the next morning good communists. It happened before, in 1933, that kind of thing. They've had plenty of practice."

"Obviously," Clark said, "you have no relatives there."

"I do," Klaus said pleasantly. "A hag of an aunt. Even Russian soldiers wouldn't go near her." And, as they moved off, he wondered, almost to himself: "What will the English do? You've never seen your own nation raped by Russians." He slipped against the window again. "If you want to drive faster, I'm not a nervous passenger."

They were out on the slip-road now, accelerating; Clark was searching into the column of traffic, looking for a gap to slot the car into.

Klaus seemed asleep already.
Clark was thinking about his daughter.

WEDNESDAY

It was a cheap hotel off Habsburger Platz. When Clark woke, he could hear the noise of a hoover down the passage, yearning and struggling. It was that which had woken him. Seven twenty. Anywhere but Germany, he reflected, and there would have been a riot if a hoover had been switched on so early. Here it was different: Everyone had already gone to work.

Klaus was in the next room, naked between the sheets. He had brought nothing with him except a small, green washbag, done up by a zip across its top. "When you'd gone to bed last night, I rang Brussels," Klaus said. His hair looked a mess. "They are moving out. All that is true. Some of them are going to Baden Baden. The Dane gave me a telephone number to ring there, from tonight." He turned his head towards the curtained window. "Is it raining?"

As Clark moved towards the window, Klaus added: "Dahlem rang the Dane yesterday. But that was anticipated. He's rung twice before." Clark drew the curtain back. It wasn't raining. Munich: A hard-drinking, solid, heavy town; a town where a man would order a big beer drawn from a pump — not a little bottle with a fancy label — and expect to be left alone while he drank it. He looked down along the street, choked with parked cars. Below him, a woman was trying to get a Mercedes into a space at the pavement, her head out of the window and peering back, to gauge the distance. A man in leather breeches and Alpine hat stood on the corner, waiting vacantly. Opposite him, vegetables were being sold on waste-land from a caravan. Small blackboards were grouped around it with the day's prices chalked on them. Clark could see the silhouette of a man deep within it, arranging Bulgarian tomatoes in pyramids on the counter.

"Dahlem is a clever boy," Klaus said. "He's calculated it all. He wants an exchange: One piece of paper for a thousand Swiss francs. He'll do a daily exchange. That's the only way he can protect himself."

"How many pieces of paper are there?"

"He won't say how many. He says he'll come every night for the exchange. He won't be able to touch him. Nobody will. If he's grabbed, you forfeit all the other pieces of paper. He'll have them hidden somewhere, in an envelope probably, with instructions for somebody to put it in the post immediately if he doesn't come back from the exchange."

They ate breakfast in the bar. Four tables had been covered in white, disposable paper table-cloths. The barman, a slight, effeminate young man, unshaven and wearing no tie, brought them a plate of cold meats and strips of cheese and black bread. Klaus ate with a fork only, folding the strips of meat and forcing them into his mouth, masticating them heavily. He didn't seem to eat bread at all. "The exchange is at midnight," he said. "We've a day to kill." He stood up, lifted a discarded morning newspaper from another table and returned with it. "I'm going to the cinema. What do you want to do? You could take a tour of the museums. The coaches run every hour from outside the railway station." He smiled. "Or you could go over to Dachau. It's only ten kilometres from Munich. They have a much more interesting film show there."

An old radio poured music into the room and the barman followed the tunes, humming between his teeth. Now he emerged with more paper table-cloths, ostentatiously turned his back on where they sat, and began spreading them, ready for lunch.

"I think you ought to go away for the day," Klaus said. "I don't think we ought to see each other. You're heavy company."

"And what the hell does that mean?"

"Just a question I keep asking myself: Why did they pick you?"

Eleven thirty. The night was arctic cold. It made the city into a tundra, each gutter a static ice-flow; the frost lay like a skin across the heaps of decayed leaves. A little steam rose from the rooftops, as damp as condensation.

Clark parked the car on the corner of Furstenrieder Strasse, at the cross-roads, in front of the Dresdner Bank. Its window was empty, save for the day's exchange rates for foreign currencies on a stand, and a triangular placard placed at the other end, with a slogan printed at an angle across it, and punctuated by an exclamation mark. Clark locked the car. Klaus was already on the pavement, looking round, professionally assessing the terrain: To one side, the tram terminus, a long, low building with a tobacco kiosk set into it and magazines on shelves within, and iron mesh drawn across the closed door. An elderly man with a Slavonic face — a guest worker, no doubt of that — was asleep on a bench, his boots placed firmly on the ground, his arms folded across his chest; asleep in spite of the cold. Drunk, Klaus thought. To the other side, the cemetery: A slate-grey wall, ten feet high and decorated, at its top, by three rows of curved red tiles. The wrought iron gates were open.

A Fiat, coming quickly down Wurmtal Strasse, traversed the tram lines, its wheels bouncing urgently, and went away into the distance. Klaus watched it go. Then they crossed the road, crossed the arc of cobblestones by the gates, and went in.

An open-sided shed had been constructed against the wall,

a place to leave bicycles, with a row of metal hoops set into the concrete base to hold their front wheels. It was empty. Klaus saw the notice board further away, with a map of the cemetery pinned to it, behind glass. He walked over. The cemetery was divided into avenues, each plot numbered. It looked like an ordnance survey map, lacking only the contour lines for height. The cemetery was level.

The cemetery was full of tall, matured trees planted so close together that their branches interlocked above, making the avenues into grottos of foliage. They seemed to press the air down and hold it in, fetid, dank and perfectly still.

A gravel path threaded between the trees away from them. The graves were set back from the path: Each headstone of a different shape and material, the last gesture of individuality; some coarse stone, some granite, some varnished wood; some symmetrical, some curved; one was half-covered in ivy, the leaves wreathed across the inscription. The names of whole families had been cut into the larger headstones, beginning with the oldest name at the top left-hand corner and going down in columns: Just names and dates. Posies of pink flowers — hardy as rock plants — were placed at the foot of many graves.

They walked forward, side by side, until they reached the intersection. The grave to the right had a thick, red candle flickering silently in a lantern beside it. They turned into avenue fourteen. It was marked by a small stone, fashioned in the shape of a headstone. The branches were lower now, and would have brushed against a tall man, standing erect; interwoven across the avenue, unfeeling hands joining together to shade the light.

They reached the pond: A small, circular pond, upraised, and with a brick wall enclosing it, knee high. The brass tap which fed it dripped insistently, single drops which fell into the water, creating ripples which enlarged briefly and died. Plastic watering cans hung on a metal frame, to be dipped into the pond and borne away to tend the posies of flowers. Three further avenues converged on the pond, two of them leading towards the heart of the cemetery; and, because they were further away from the street lamps on the road, they were dark, and the candles, the headstones and the trees blended into a satanic curtain.

"It's here," Klaus said. He regarded the pond. "I wonder why it's not frozen over. The water is probably heated. Germans think of everything." He turned to see whether Clark appreciated the little joke; sat on the brick wall and dipped his hand into the water, disturbing it. "Yes, heated." He dried his hand against the side of the flying jacket. "You go and wait up there, along that avenue. Don't try and hide. He'll have watched us come in together."

Clark positioned himself twenty yards away, beside an ornate headstone, with marble angels playing mute trumpets, and a single name enscribed beneath the angels in Gothic script: Sabine Adelmann, 1962 — 1967. A child. Perhaps the mother came each Sunday and stood before it; perhaps the father came with a trowel and trimmed the borders of the grave. There was no inscription, no dedication beside the name; the dates proclaimed the tragedy.

He shrugged. How many had he seen like that, by the rice fields beyond Kaesong, the cluster of simple bamboo crosses, the cross-members lashed to the stems, and just numbers branded into them, with hot irons, because there had been no time for the recording of names; the little heaps of dry, reddish soil where the bodies lay and the group of women before them, standing together, taking warmth and comfort from each other and the communal grief shared, the communal grief spread.

Now Klaus leant against a tree-trunk next to the pond. If he had been a schoolboy, his posture would have been called slovenly; insolent, even; and he would have been admonished. His hands were deep in his pockets. He scuffed his feet in the gravel, as if he was very bored.

Ten minutes and nothing.

"Christ it's cold," Clark called to him. He looked no notice.

A church bell tolled midnight, each toll long and precise, flattening itself against the night sky. A helicopter passed overhead as the last toll sounded, its blades cutting at the stillness.

The midnight toll: It could not have been a summons to worship at that hour, nor even a cry for the sinners. It was just marking the time.

Klaus lifted the brown envelope marked: ADN Bank, and transferred it from one pocket to another.

They both heard the footsteps on the gravel, short, sharp footsteps, becoming louder.

They both saw the hooded figure, down the avenue, the hood concealing almost all the face and the dark cape reaching down to below the knees.

Klaus was still leaning. He turned his head but made no other move except to bring his hands from his pockets — the envelope was in the left — to demonstrate that he held no weapon. He let the figure come to him; watched the hesitation a short distance away, perhaps four or five yards; beyond reach. The candles quivered among the shrubs, sentinels in the shadow.

Klaus said something in German and held out the envelope, waist high. The figure came forward again, nervously, like a rabbit instinctively and helplessly fearing assault.

They stood, facing each other. Klaus, very gently, reached out a hand and pushed the hood back, a gesture which was almost a caress. It fell back, crumpled about the shoulders.

Then he smiled.

It was a girl.

THURSDAY

Klaus made a telephone call in the morning. Clark assumed it was to the Dane. Then they drank coffee in the hotel bar and just waited. Klaus said: "I wonder what the receptionist out there would say if we brought a couple of women back here. She might not object. She must have seen that before. I know a place in the centrum. . . ."

But Clark shook his head.

The man came in the afternoon. He looked like a civil servant as he stood at the reception desk, asking for them. The girl lifted her head and nodded towards the bar.

They sat at a table, watching the children's programmes on the television. A young man with very long hair and a sweater plucked fitfully at a guitar and sang ditties.

He did not give his name. He volunteered nothing. He only showed Klaus his plastic identification disk, encased in clear plastic so that the legend within could not be altered. He took the single piece of paper which Klaus had got in the cemetery and placed it with great care in an envelope; sealed the envelope and made Klaus sign across the seal in a biro he held out.

Bureaucrats, Clark thought savagely. Bloody, wretched bureaucrats.

The man stood erect, turned and walked stiffly away, as if he was guarding his dignity.

"They've found out some more things about Dahlem,"

Klaus said. "The Dane told me this morning. He said it was OK to tell you." The slight, small turn of the knife; the calculated denigration, so that their relationship would retain its present status: Klaus making all the running.

"Six years he works for them, four of those years in some kind of position — and now they get curious about him." Klaus shook his head. "You know what he wanted? He wanted his share. He wanted the money because he was taught to want the money. Every hoarding, every goddam TV programme screamed the message at him: Big holidays, new clothes, luxury apartments, fast cars. Dear God, the poor little sod believed it. You know what he was paid? I could show you the figures. It wasn't so goddam much for a German, even if he was working in Belgium. He drives an old Volkswagen, a really old one. Nine years at least. That was all he could afford when he passed the test."

Klaus leant back, expansive and sure of himself, propounding the theory he had created. "Sure, that's how it is: He was taught to want things, and when they weren't give to him, he went out to get them for himself. The ethics of the bloody age were on his side. But that's only part of it." He leant forward now, his face close to Clark's. "They've turned up his medical record. Apparently they're kept in a different department, for pension purposes. So it took a little longer to locate, especially with the exodus from Brussels pending. They had a doctor's report on him, just a standard medical when he joined, and also some photostats of his national health card. God knows where they got those from." Klaus raised a hand to brush away some hair which had fallen across his eyebrow. "Dahlem was impotent. A disease in childhood. I forget the technical name. It was in Latin and I didn't understand it, anyway. Neither did the Dane." Klaus leant back. "A eunuch. A bloody, childlike eunuch." He stood up. "I'm going out to buy some shampoo. While I'm away, you think about that."

Midnight, and the rain again, driving rain slanting into the branches of the cemetery, buffeting them, being absorbed by them, then falling from them in lone drops. It pattered on the gravel, the sound of rats' feet on dry granary floorboards; it ran down the headstones in rivulets.

"I'd have preferred another frost," Klaus said. He was under the same tree, partially sheltered but already his hair was wet, and the sodden strands stuck to the base of his neck.

She came the same way. She wore the same hood. She lowered her head in recognition. Klaus held up the envelope. She couldn't know it was empty, not until it was opened. He'd put some notepaper in it, in the hotel, to make it look thicker. She went close to him, blind in her trust because it had all worked the night before.

He grasped her as she reached out for the envelope, in both hands, letting the envelope fall onto the gravel, by his feet; held her like a doll, turned her, her arm locked behind her back.

"Dahlem," he called out, down the avenue.

His voice echoed among the headstones; melted into the falling rain.

"Dahlem."

He had the knife out, at her throat, and he moved her in an arc so that she could be seen from all angles; and from all the avenues.

"Dahlem."

There was no reply, no movement except the ebbing wind, spreading the branches and the falling rain.

They stood blended together with the street lamps from Furstenrieder Strasse reaching meekly to their feet.

He pushed her forward, raising her arm behind her back so that she stooped; back down avenue fourteen, left, and towards the cemetery gates. Clark followed at a discreet distance.

They went through the gates, out onto the arc of cobbles flanking the street. They were near a lamp standard, and Klaus rotated the blade of the knife so that the light caught it, caught the texture of the steel.

"Dahlem," he called again.

The girl was breathless, and her dark hair lay over her face, the rain falling on it; the hand which Klaus held was small and as fragile as a piece of bone china, the skin white from the pressure where he gripped it, the slender fingers crushed, as if they were reeds woven together.

He forced her down onto her knees.

He's mad, Clark thought, standing ten paces away, just within the wrought iron gates. Any passing motorist will see him; will stop to help the girl, or go on and telephone the police.

The cobblestones cut at her knees, grating and tearing the fabric of the nylons.

"Dahlem," he shouted, loud and careless. "I'll break her arm." He pressed her forward, and she cried out in pain, her head contorted backward, her hair spread.

"Arthur," she murmured, her mouth open. "Please help me. Please. The pain is so great."

But the man didn't come.

They waited a long moment, then went back, all three, into the cemetery, Klaus still holding the girl's arm, but loosely. They were near the notice board.

"Where is he?" Klaus asked.

"I don't know."

He released her arm so that, for an instant, she was off-balance; struck her with his closed fist in the stomach. She sank away from him, doubled up.

"Where is he?"

She shook her head. The answer was the same: She didn't know.

He moved towards her. Dribbles of rain were running down the glass case which held the map. She lifted her eyes.

"That's enough," Clark said. "Don't touch her again." Klaus swivelled. He had the knife out. It was a Boy Scout knife with a wooden handle and a chip in the blade, because it had been used for opening tins of food. "I'll disembowel you," he said to Clark. "I'll spread your guts on the gravel if you get in the way." He held the knife low, knee level and probing forward and up, the point of the blade towards Clark's stomach.

The girl said: "We had an apartment in Schwabing. But he said that if anything went wrong, he would run away. He won't be there."

She was crying convulsively. It could have been the pain; it could have been that she'd just lost Dahlem.

As they came out, Klaus said to Clark: "You're lucky. Not everybody gets killed in a cemetery." He was smiling.

They sat in the car, the girl and Klaus in the back.

"Run where?"

"He didn't say. Ever." The coat had fallen away from her lap, revealing the nylons torn at the knee, the perforated skin and a little blood, already congealing.

"You must have talked about it. You must have had tickets for the travel. I mean, he was going to take you with him." He looked at her knee as he spoke. It was an odd thing to say, because it implied that Dahlem wasn't going to take her; would use her to run the errands and then discard her, as he had done. It was the first attempt to turn her.

"He thought the exchange would work. He thinks that everything he does will work."

"Aeroplane tickets?" She shook her head.

"Did he have a passport on him?"

"Yes. He carried it at all times."

"Was he in the Volkswagen?"

She hesitated.

"I'll hurt you again," Klaus said.

Clark, silent and unmoving at the steering wheel, was on the point of turning round. But she sensed that Clark couldn't protect her. Klaus had the knife, and Klaus was very close, their shoulders almost together.

"Yes, he had the Volkswagen."

Her face was drawn and pallid in the street lamps; ethereal and unreal, like an illuminated death mask. She drew her knees up and arranged the coat over them so that the blood might not be seen, an instinctive, feminine gesture to restore her appearance. The toes of the black, patent-leather shoes were scuffed; the same tearing as of the skin of the knees.

"He thought you were a whore," Klaus said. "Otherwise he would have come and got you. Either that, or he's a coward."

"Arthur is a pacifist," the girl said, very softly, as if Dahlem was worth defending and now she was going to defend him. "He believes a man does not need to carry a knife in his pocket to be a man." She twisted her head and regarded Klaus, suddenly, without fear.

"The papers," Klaus said. He wound the window down to let in the cool night air; a little rain spat at his face. "How many papers were there, and where did he keep them?"

"He had them hidden somewhere. He said it would be better for me not to know where. He considered me. They weren't at the flat."

"He considered himself. He sent you. He didn't tell you because he was better off if you were ignorant. Then you couldn't tell anybody anything." He waited for her reaction; found none. "But he had to get that first paper, yesterday, for the exchange. And again today."

"He went out in the afternoon. He was away for about an hour. I didn't time him. Of course. Why should I? He came back with the envelope which I gave to you."

"Look," Klaus said, "you might feel something for Dahlem. You might be crazy for him. God knows why, but you might just be. But this is important. Don't you listen to the news bulletins? The papers are more important than he knows. He was a clerk. He knows what the papers are worth, but he hasn't the mentality to see the consequences of the papers."

"How do you know about his mentality?" Again the defence.

"Because he was a clerk. If he'd been Einstein, he'd have risen further than that."

She shrugged. It was true. She knew nothing.

"We'll go back to the hotel. I'll ring the Dane and tell him to set it all in motion: Frontier checks, airport checks, autobahn patrols looking for the Volkswagen. We can't do that by ourselves. If we went to the police here and asked for that facility, they'd laugh in our faces. Then we'll go to Schwabing and look at the apartment. We won't find anything there except dirty underwear, but we'll have to go all the same. The Dane savours that, you know. Thoroughness. Christ, we're all civil servants, and that's the truth."

He sat back into the seat as Clark moved off, closed his eyes and let the wind from the open window play on his hair, distending it.

Schwabing at two in the morning, and they passed through a wide, empty park. "It's called the Englischer Garten," Klaus observed, opening his eyes momentarily. "I hope you feel at home." Clark grunted something. A scenic lake was broken by some small islands. Rowing boats had been moored by a wooden jetty; the wind disturbed the water and they jostled together. Schwabing: An inner suburb, favoured by students. Rebuilt, clean and modern with tall houses, fussy in the Bavarian way.

The girl directed him to Lunebergerstrasse, a side-road with three-storey houses and no front gardens, just the pavement and parked cars at the kerb.

"It's up there," she said. "Number 101. On the right side."

It was a cross-roads. Clark parked and all three of them got out. Klaus looked round, precisely as he had done at the cemetery, on the first night. The girl pushed at the heavy, oaken door and they were in a courtyard, ducking beneath a washing line, walking on into the building through an open entrance. She pressed a luminous button and the lights sprang on. Up the stone staircase. The time switch was ticking, set just long enough to allow someone to gain the third floor, then extinguish the lights automatically.

The first floor. She had a key in her coat pocket, on a piece of string. "We had to get it specially cut," she said. "The landlord would only give us one, and Arthur needed that."

She fumbled with it and had to turn it twice before the lock opened. They were in a bare, uncarpeted room. Klaus closed the door. "Don't go near the window," he said. He turned to Clark. "Man in a Skoda, Austrian plates. See him?" Clark said nothing. "Other side of the road, beyond the street lamp. In the shadow. He was smoking. Very stupid." Klaus went to the window himself; it was covered in net curtain, faded and soiled by the suns of forgotten summers. "Any back exit here?" The girl whispered no; she was exhausted and wanted no more trouble. "He's still there. He's been told just to wait, and that's what he's doing." He motioned towards the girl. "Come with me." And to Clark: "Stay here. You stay here."

Klaus and the girl went out. The lights were off. He pressed the button on the landing, walked quickly down the stairway and back across the courtyard, the girl following; drew back the oaken door. "When we get out on the pavement, we're going to hold hands and walk very slowly. You put your head against my shoulder. Act like we're lovers. That shouldn't be so hard. You must have done it with

Dahlem."

They did come out holding hands and wandered along towards the cross-roads. The rain had stopped, leaving the road glistening. The Skoda was fifty yards away, on the other side; settled in front of a clothing shop, the naked and unadorned dummies locked in poses, the narrow arms at artificial angles, the fingers splayed, ghosts in the lamp-light; and one draped in a heavy fur coat, arrested in the act of stepping forward. They crossed the road, their hands held tight because the girl wanted to turn and run. The Skoda was up in front of them now, five or six parked cars between them. They moved past a doctors; the black plaque on the wall by his door embellished, in flowing letters, with his name and qualifications and visiting hours. Three cars away, they heard the Skoda's engine being switched on, a churning, a coughing, then a humming. Klaus released her hand. The Skoda had begun to nose uncertainly out, like an insect probing with antannae, because the space between the car in front of it and the car behind it was not great enough.

The girl stood away.

Klaus had the knife out, the arm which held it down at his side, the blade against the seam of his trouser leg. He was out in the road as the car gathered momentum, coming towards him; but it was still travelling slowly. They all knew it, the inescapable, mechanical reality: Skodas have no acceleration. He swayed as the car reached him, as a bullfighter might have done; grasped the handle of the driver's door as it brushed against him, and tried to wrench it open; but the impetus dragged him forward and as the door opened it pressed him away, drew him downward. Still he clung, both hands locked to the chromium handle. The knife was back down the road, where he had released it. His legs were spread, and the gathering speed twisted his whole body, drawing it against the side of the car.

Clark, at the window, cried: Christ, Christ, it's going to

take him underneath, under the back wheels. It's going to crush him. . . .

The heel of one shoe caught the surface of the road, and the whole foot was thrown up.

Then he fell, at the instant his fingers released the handle; fell away, and the flying jacket was bunched around his waist, and blood was in his hair; and he lay, wrecked, in the same lamp-light; lay still, face down, both arms beneath the body as if they had been dismembered.

The girl screamed; covered her mouth with her hands; and did not move towards him.

Clark thought of Echtmann.

FRIDAY

Klaus woke shortly after eight. The girl was at the bedside with a chilled, moist flannel, leaning into him and holding it against his forehead. The flying jacket had been removed but he still wore his shirt, unbuttoned; dried blood lay down the front of it and some had fallen onto the pillow in a crescent. It had seeped into the material, and expanded, purple-tinged, angry stains of differing shapes. Klaus lifted his head, surveyed the apartment — the animal instinct to know where he was, to fix the surroundings — and said brutally: "Dahlem must have played with you on this very bed, my dear. And now here I am." His head drifted back, as if he were reluctant to release control of it; his eyes were already closed.

The girl called out and Clark came; looked down at Klaus.

"Asleep," the girl said. She clutched the flannel in both hands, solemn and supplicant as a hymn book. The nail varnish on her fingers had chipped: Broken tiles.

"Hey," Klaus said from far away. "Hey, hey, hey." He had begun to sweat. The stubble on his chin was dark and rough: An untilled field. "I'm only resting."

"You should be certified for trying a stunt like that," Clark said, pragmatically and without feeling.

"I know. I should have got into our car and rammed the Skoda instead. It came to me in the night. I thought I had a fever, but I didn't. Completely lucid, like a replay on film. All the details were intact: The noise of the engine, the tread on the tyres, the feel of the door handle. OK. We should have rammed him; but you know what I kept thinking in the night? What if he'd been an ordinary motorist?"

He had begun to turn his head from side to side, a slow, rocking motion, irrational and inexplicable. "You never thought of that. You assumed" . . . and his lips parted. The smile. The rotten, stinking, self-satisfied smile. "You didn't even see the Skoda in the first place." He twisted his head away from the thinned daylight filtering through the lace curtain; it could have been hurting his eyes. "It wasn't Dahlem in there. I saw the face. Not his. Austrian plates. Vienna number, a big, yellow W in front of it. It was somebody from the east. They're looking for him, too."

"What was in the papers he took?" Clark had moved closer to the bed. "I've a right to know. I want to know." He paused. "What were the papers about?"

A soft smile now, a different degree of self-satisfaction. Klaus had brought the older man to this. The anticipated conquest. His tongue, far into the cavity of his mouth, scoured the teeth, jagged as broken glass, for a little moisture. "Ask the Dane. He'll tell you to go to hell. He won't say it like that. He'll be much more diplomatic. He'll couch it in the proper phrases, to reassure you. But the message will be the same." He closed his mouth. His tongue was moving behind the cheeks, distending them; the same search for moisture. "I'll tell you one thing: As a chauffeur, you're very steady." He turned his head again, towards the window; now he might have welcomed the light. Get me some water to drink. Now."

"And I'll tell you one thing," Clark said. The girl had gone away with the flannel, gone back into the living room and placed herself close to the telephone, on a plain wooden chair. She might have expected it to ring at any moment.

Her withdrawal might have been feminine prudence, because she wished to avoid a scene between the two men; it might have been pragmatism, because she really did expect the phone to ring, and she wanted to be the first to answer it.

"On the news this morning," Clark said. "On the radio. The Russians have concluded a pact with Finland. The Finns have been an unofficial satellite for years; they put a hand up, and rang Moscow, before they went to the toilet, apparently. As bad as that. But now some Finnish delegation representing their labour party has actually been to Moscow and signed all kinds of things. All dressed up in the mumbo-jumbo they use: A mutual economic and defence agreement. That was the phrase. Can you hear me?" Klaus nodded, the unshaven chin dipping towards the throat. "Russian troops are moving into Finland as part of it. There isn't going to a Mannerheim line, they aren't going to defend the frozen lakes this time. The tanks are skirting Helsinki, staying on the circular motorway they're grouping at a place called Turku on the Baltic. I'd never heard of it before. But it's got full naval facilities, and it's directly opposite Stockholm." He moved even closer to the bed; wondered whether he should sit, on the iron rim, avoiding Klaus's lean legs beneath the blankets; decided against, and remained erect, maintaining the posture of a soldier. "They're going to take it all this time. The Swedes will turn up their hands and cry: Neutral. Too bad. They're going to take it all. *All.*"

But Klaus was asleep.

Thirty minutes later, Klaus murmured — and each of the words might have come from deep within him, pressing through a sedative, though he had been given none — "Did you ring Baden Baden?"

Clark said: "Yes." It was not a simple statement because the thread of the conversation was altered away from him.

"Dahlem: Has he been sighted?"

"Nothing," Clark said. "Except he parked the Volkswagen outside the police station in Viktualienmarkt — if you pronounce it like that." Klaus nodded; a solemn movement worthy of a clergyman, granting absolution; bestowing assent. "He went into the police station and asked the duty officer if they could keep an eye on it during the night. He said there are so many thieves about these days. Then he went away."

Klaus opened his eyes suddenly. "He's crazy," he said. "I told you that already: He's crazy."

Lunch-time. The girl had begun to cook a meal. She had been out alone to do the shopping; had returned with some meat burgers, a tin of carrots, and potatoes in a clear plastic bag. They would have come from the caravan, down the street. Klaus was awake, his head propped against the upraised pillow.

"Did you give the Dane our number here?" Klaus's hands rested along the white, covering sheet, equidistant and against the legs. The right wrist was bruised. The welts had risen, a mottling of blue and black.

"Of course."

One might expect competence; little else, perhaps, but competence, at least.

"Why did you let the girl go alone?"

"Shut up."

"You trusted her. You trusted her because she's a woman. You're as stupid as the man in the Skoda: Smoking at night." He discussed in a detached way, evaluating the technical error with no particular malice. "Bloody British. You'll all have to grow up one day." And then: "When the tanks come, up from Dover — skirting Canterbury, staying on the circular motorway — you'll grow up." He might have relished — even in the fleeting, sunken moment — the prospect. Whether that was a personal matter between himself and Clark — created by the age difference — or whether it was the inbred, instinctive memory of his own national rape, Clark could not say. It might even have been the cultivated cynicism of youth, asserting itself and denigrating the reality it did not comprehend; it might have been simply that Klaus was a hard man.

The flat was home ground now; first base. The single bedroom, with just the iron bed and two suitcases, one for Dahlem and one for the girl, clothes neatly folded in piles within them, shirts and ties and summer dresses, the underwear discreetly placed beneath; and a threadbare, worn, exhausted, lime green carpet; worn back to the thread underneath at certain, strategic points, where the footfalls had been most frequent, across the years; and the wash-basin in a corner, the two metal bars under it — one at each side — draped with soiled hand towels; and the lounge, larger, with no carpet at all, but only a reddish linoleum, and a television set placed on the lap of one of the wooden chairs; and a red telephone beside another chair; and another chair, naked, by itself, towards the window, turned and left, neither here nor there. It would have to be moved again before anybody sat on it. And an electric fire, a false electric fire with a facade moulded into the form of logs which glowed, red, but more livid than the linoleum; and a blocked-off chimney stack; and a petite table, coated in veneer, one corner broken away; like the girl's finger nails.

Klaus got up in the afternoon and dressed himself awkwardly. His rib cage seemed to hurt and, in a kind of ritual, he pressed each rib to ascertain whether it was broken or not. His left ankle had swelled down to the heel. The girl had stuck a plaster over his forehead, a rectangular plaster, making him look absurdly crippled, an invalid ready for pity and mercy. He came into the living room slowly; he was nursing his body and sudden movement would bring back the pain in the ribs. He selected the chair by the window, carried it to the other chairs and sat; his feet bare, the toes mis-shapen, the webbing between them pronouned, a prehensile birthmark, to be viewed only by those who saw him naked.

The girl had the flying jacket over her knees and was carefully sewing the shoulder where the road had torn it. Clark was washing the lunch plates in the hand-basin.

"Who did he contact in the east?" Klaus asked.

The girl looked up. "I have no idea." The needle was poised in her left hand, the thread hanging from it. "I do not think he had any relatives there. If he did, he did not speak of them."

"Not relatives. Contacts. Did he make any phone calls to the east? Did he meet anybody you didn't recognise? Did he arrange a rendez-vous?"

She shook her head. She had begun to sew again, mechanically, pressing the point of the needle into the fabric of the jacket, forcing it down, forcing it up again, dragging the thread through and then drawing the two sides of the crevice together.

"He must have," Klaus said. "Otherwise, how did they know he was in Munich — and here, in this flat?" He shifted his feet. "They were waiting last night."

She shook her head again, the pitiful, submissive motion of a woman adrift. "He was secret about everything. He told me it was better for me not to know of such things."

Klaus stood up and wandered to the window, almost limping; brushed away the lace curtain and surveyed the crossroads; checked each of the parked cars. They were all empty. "They've gone, whoever they were," he said, almost inaudibly. He came back, twisted the wooden chair and positioned it closer to the girl. "Leave the jacket and look at me." Her little hands stopped; her face was raised, obedient; frightened again. She had put on some eyeshadow, bluish in colour: Her eyes were sad, because she had tried to make herself attractive and failed. She wore a dress without sleeves, a summer dress, discordant in the winter. Her arms were pallid and thin; the bone structure appeared brittle, like the legs of a chicken, and Klaus thought, just then, that if he had twisted just a little harder outside the cemetery, the arm he held would have snapped; not broken, not fractured; snapped.

"We'll go through it right from the beginning," Klaus said. She searched his eyes for a little pity, a little understanding; found nothing except indifference. They both knew that he would hurt her again, if that was needed. He had imagined that she was sewing the jacket to please him; to establish some sort of relationship through the kindness which would preclude further violence. But as he looked at her, he knew he was wrong. She'd been used to mothering Dahlem; she was that kind of woman.

So they began. It lasted an hour, Clark walking up and down the far side of the room, listening and reflecting in silence. Klaus was thorough. Clark was surprised. He posed questions, not as an art in itself — he disregarded insinuation, innuendo; had no wish to lead her up trifling cul-de-sacs, turn her back on herself, make her contradict herself. He regarded questions as vehicles for gathering information. Occasionally, he would say: "Explain more fully." That was all.

In the end, the girl said: "Arthur was impotent."

"I know. It is in his medical records." He took no satisfaction from the fact that he knew. "It is clearly marked on his card, in red ink, years ago, and signed by a doctor."

"A medical card!" Her hand lay across the jacket, her legs crossed. "Of course you would see it like that. A disability, which would affect his pension rights." Her hands moved, gathering one fallen arm of the jacket and folding it absently below her hands, then smoothing it, as if that might have comforted her. "He tried to make love. That was the most terrible thing. He tried." Her eyes were closed. "He bought lotions and ..." and she reached for the word, the single word, forced it out because it was, alone and unadorned, the enshrining of dreadful nights and the personal memory of them, now bared before a violent stranger . . . "contraptions."

She turned her head away, though his reaction was unimportant: Her eyes were still closed. "They were ugly and shaming. When he bought them, they gave him brochures; manuals of instruction. I begged him to forget all this. I begged him. He used to lie and sweat in that bed over there because the desire was so strong and he could never be released from it. He stroked me with nervous hands and cried. He pressed his face into the pillow, so that I might not hear him crying, and feigned sleep. I could not help him. I asked him just to love me. But he said I would go with other men and, when that happened, he would destroy himself. He used to stand there, in a corner, and tell me it would all be better like that." Still the hand moved along the sleeve, the fingers running over the folds and creases in the fabric. "I don't know what he stole and I don't care." The weakness was becoming anger and, with it, uncaring courage; together, they consumed the consequences. "He had a right to what he stole. They insulted him in Brussels. They treated him like a messenger boy. I wonder if that is on his medical card." She stood, letting the jacket slip away and fall to the floor where it lay, as wrecked as Klaus had been, inside it, the night before. "They made him run errands. They made him fetch the coffee, even for the most junior of the typists. They laughed at him, but never to his face. He knew. He sensed everything. And even then, he did his work. None of them ever complained about his work."

They were watching each other. Clark had stopped and stood, motionless, near the closed door.

"They were just like you. They hated him because he was not one of them — he didn't make foul jokes, he didn't go out drinking, he didn't. . . ." Her whole body was convulsed by the anger. "And now you come and torture me. You don't understand suffering. You think suffering it getting knocked down by a car, and having a plaster on your forehead. You're half a man, you, a bastard, a clever, arrogant bastard, a Jew-baiter. You would defecate on the graves, you."

She moved towards Klaus, tears swelling in her eyes, the little hands clenched into fists. She tried stupidly to strike his face. He seized the arm and held it, away from him, like a man holding a rifle and presenting arms. She twisted her head to one side. "Bastard," she cried. And again: "Bastard." But the second time, the words died away, into her tears, an echo passing across dried lips; a useless, empty gesture against his strength. He levered her down into the chair, released the arm. She covered her face. One foot rested on the flying jacket, the other on the floor.

Then the phone rang.

Clark stooped to where the receiver lay and lifted it, listened for a moment, repeated "Yes" several times, and said to Klaus: "It's for you." Klaus rose and went slowly to the telephone. He, too, listened, and when the conversation was ended, said: "Dahlem was seen at the Welt Bank. He had deposited something in their vaults, and went to collect it this morning. He was there waiting when they opened." Klaus smiled, that particular, bitter smile he could create. "He's gone now. Christ knows where."

THE SECOND WEEK:
ENDS AND BEGINNINGS

SATURDAY

They waited in the flat. The rain had come back, battering limply at the window-panes, borne on the wind. Klaus moved round the room incessantly; the constriction troubled him. He paused from time to time at the window itself; paused long enough to survey the greying rooftops, glistening in the dull afternoon light. From another flat came the sound of a radio commentary, almost hysterical, of a football match, the rise and fall of the commentator's voice reflecting the ebb and flow of the game.

"The police will pick him up," Clark said. "Then we can all go home."

"The police are stupid," Klaus said. "He parked the Volkswagen outside the police station and they promised to watch over it." He was at the window. It might have been a hospital window: Vistas of freedom. Opposite, an old man was boarding over his ground-floor windows. He had a heap of planks on the pavement, a hammer in his hand and nails in a cotton bag at his waist. His wife hovered close by. The wind caught her apron and she held it down with her hands, as she might have done a skirt. "They're getting ready," Klaus observed.

"Getting ready for what?" It was Clark who spoke.

"The occupation."

The girl was asleep on the bed, fully-dressed.

The man had finished the first window; backed away from it and regarded the criss-cross of planks nailed to the window frame; came forward and tugged at them to make sure they were secure. Further up the road, a silver coloured BMW was being parked. The driver got out and opened the boot. It held three cardboard boxes of tinned food. He carried each laboriously into the opened door of his house; the laying-in of stores.

"Where would he go?" Klaus mused. The girl was breathing heavily. "Railway stations? Too obvious. The airport? Obvious again. Hitch a lift? His mind doesn't work in that direction. Hire a car? Too dangerous. He'd have to produce his driving licence with his name on it. Hotels? That's more interesting. I thought of asking the Dane to get the police to check them all. There can't be that many in Munich. He has to sleep somewhere, wash, shave, go to the toilet. He'd been wearing the same shirt for two days at least — unless he's bought another one. His shaving kit is here, toothpaste, toothbrush. He could be in a derelict house, with the tramps. But they distrust outsiders, and if he's so damn prim and proper, I can't see him lying down on a straw bed next to a hairy old tramp." Klaus needed the monologue; he needed to talk aloud, exploring the options. "He could have bought a tent and pitched it in the woods. That would make the most sense. Cold but safe. The thing is, he hasn't much time. He contacted the east. Echtmann relayed that back. By the way, wasn't Echtmann due to make his run recently?" He turned to Clark, and Clark had no idea how much he knew; whether it was a new taunt. Clark let it go. Klaus turned back. The man had begun on the second window, his wife gone indoors. "Planks. The old fool. He should use masking tape to prevent the glass shattering. Anybody knows that." He paused, to alter the direction of the monologue. "I've been thinking about the girl, too. We can use her. She's the bait. Maybe." He sighed. "He must have felt something for her. Even if he is crazy."

"He didn't feel much before, at the cemetery. He just

cleared off."

"Because he trusted our ethics. He's seen them in Brussels, the harmless people; he doesn't think we do things like that."

"But he saw you hurting the girl."

Klaus had lost interest in the conversation. He was watching the old man struggling with the planks.

The call was at five. The football match was over, the inquest on it was over, and there was a measure of silence when the telephone rang. Klaus seized it. The Dane. Dahlem had called again; he'd rung Brussels, but the automatic re-routing of calls was in operation now. At least, the Dane observed with some distaste, the Belgians have granted us that facility.

Dahlem wanted another exchange. He wanted the girl. He wanted to go and live in peace somewhere; on the edge of a lake in a log cabin, apparently.

"He wants the girl to go over the Austrian frontier, where she will be protected by the neutrality of that country; then he will exchange the papers. When the girl crosses the frontier, she is to register at the Hotel Liegnitz, opposite the railway station, in Innsbruck. He will telephone her there in the morning, to satisfy himself that she is safe and well. Then he will give me details of where the papers are. I commended him. You know he was always careful about details." The Dane hesitated. Klaus stood, the telephone wire stretched to its utmost. "I propose that Clark accompanies the girl, and that you remain in Munich and collect the papers. I have thought a great deal about this. The papers are more important that he is. When you have the papers, go to Innsbruck. That is where Dahlem will go, to be with the girl."

"He'll have worked all that out, too."

"No doubt. No doubt. It is important also that we have the papers here as soon as possible . . . to assess their extent. Perhaps Clark and the girl ought to leave immediately. It is not such a long drive, via Garmisch and Seefeld. I have consulted the maps here. But the crossing may be difficult. There is talk of the Austrians closing the frontiers, as the Brenner was closed, to protect their neutrality. Something else." The Dane hesitated again. Perhaps he was using Klaus; perhaps Klaus was his protege, the kind of man he would have wished himself to have been: Slightly arrogant, slightly rugged — if there hadn't been the war, and the four years in England, waiting, useless; and the rebuilding after.

"We have interviewed Dahlem's mother again. He hasn't contacted her at all, which one might have expected. He used to send her money each month, but he hasn't this time. It was very strange, she said, he is always so careful and never forgets. She doesn't know exactly what he's done. She didn't know anything about the girl. She lives in Dortmund. Dahlem's father was a bus driver, but he died five years ago, so she has nothing but his pension and a state pension. Her apartment smells of cats, I am told. Don't be too zealous, and read things into that, will you?" The Dane might have been smiling. Klaus had a different sense of humour and didn't think it was funny at all. Clark was listening, trying to catch the drift of the conversation. "All his personal effects are still with his mother. He did not bring them to Brussels. She has even kept his school satchel. This is why I thought he would have contacted her: The homing instinct. But he hasn't. He's adrift. He may be armed. It is a mistake to assume he will not be. That is another reason why I considered that you, not Clark, should accompany the girl to Innsbruck. By the way, he was in the choir. His voice didn't break. We all know why." Klaus did laugh this time. The Dane was almost offended. "He hated contact sports, too. He tried to join a girl's netball team at school." The girl was beginning to wake. "Something else. I won't lecture you about urgency. The Americans have sent a delegation to Moscow. They tried to keep it quiet, but that is seemingly impossible there. The newspapers haven't heard yet, but that can only be a matter of hours. The Americans are very disturbed. Their people here with us have been agitated for several days. At first, they assumed the tanks were . . . were a tactical thing. A prolonged night exercise. You know that the Russians have constant manoeuvres in East Germany, all the year round. The Americans thought it was a rehearsal. They don't understand the mentality. When the tanks stayed ten kilometres from the frontier, they all went onto a green alert. They didn't consult us, they simply did it. Now they're going to Moscow."

"It's Chamberlain again."

"Possibly. Now send Clark to Innsbruck."

The girl was sitting on the bed. Klaus gave her a precis of the situation, no more, and she began to pack her suitcase. A large, light blue case of synthetic material bound by two leather straps with buckles. A single label had been stuck to one side. Malaga is sunshine, it said, not even evoking the memory of a holiday past, but an advertisement. Then she and Clark left in the car. Klaus was putting on the kettle when they went; he said nothing, made no sign, simply stirred the coffee into the cup, his back to them.

Nightfall, and the snow had started, melting onto the pavements which were still moist from the rain.

They skirted an open market, rows of canvas stalls across a square, and bare, leafless trees between them, lit by fairy lights, draped on wire, like necklaces. It was full of women, jostling together down all the alley-ways, pushing towards only those stalls which had food and winter clothing; a sea of upraised hands reached at the goods, branches bending in the night wind. There was a subdued undercurrent of chaos and tension. Half a dozen policemen were trying to force a path towards some distant, unseen incident but the press of people caught and swallowed them, and the blue, peaked caps were spread back.

Clark had slowed the car. The girl sat next to him, looking

straight ahead, away from the market. Her suitcase rested, upright, on the back seat.

Beyond the market, darkened buildings were lost in the falling snow.

"Over there." Clark indicated a single stall, on the edge of the others, and a large woman, grotesque in the fairy lights, gesticulating against the owner of the stall. "Ten marks," she cried. "You've doubled the price." But Clark was looking at the fingers of the small child, sunk into the folds of her coat, the face nestling to her. Two of the policemen tried to turn back and reach the woman, to support or reprimand her but, in turning, they were scattered further.

"Oh God," Clark said gently. He began to move the car away.

"They all know what to do," he said. "Hoard food, buy clothing. They don't care about anything else." The crowd was eddying past a stall selling brooms and hand brushes and plastic trays for cutlery, ignoring it.

In Marienplatz, vehicles had been abandoned where they stood. A police car, its siren wailing against the wind, stood in the middle of the square, a lonely, disregarded sentinel. The snow was beginning to lie. Clark looked away to a queue at a bus stop, the first few standing under the metal canopy of the shelter, the rest lined back outside it, their arms full. Food and clothes. Nothing else. Nothing else, he noted clinically, except a young man nursing a guitar, his hands folded protectively over it to keep the snow from the strings.

He had seen this before: The rush for self-preservation. Not in Europe. He was not old enough for that. It was very odd, because the faces were just the same; the effect was just the same, glazing the eyes, shortening the tempers.

"It was on the news, the unrest," Clark said. They were at traffic lights, held by the red. The windscreen wipers scraped in front of them. "You were asleep."

She looked at him. Perhaps she was starting to trust him.

"A special news bulletin. They interrupted the programme for it. We always judge the gravity of an event by that particular criteria. . . ." He waited for her reaction. Nothing. "The Russian tanks have come forward again. They were ten kilometres from the frontier. Now it's five kilometres. That's three miles in my language; 15 minutes for tanks to traverse it." The traffic lights changed to green and he edged nervously forward. Three cars went immediately across him, one after another; went across on the red. He halted and looked studiously both ways to make sure there were no more; then advanced.

As they passed close to the police car, empty, its windows wound down, they could hear a strident voice on the intercom giving orders or requesting information. Still the snow fell.

"Will they come?" She had turned to Clark.

He was drawn, helplessly, between the truth and the lies. The Dane had said only: If it comforts you, the grass will grow on the bombsites and the children will play with rag balls among the broken masonry. . . .

"They're so strong they don't care if they give us warning," he said. "They're dispensed with surprise. They no longer need that." She might have been going to pose a further question then. "I've a daughter," Clark said. "I've a wife, too, but. . . ." His hands rested easily on the steering wheel. "My daughter is fifteen now. . . ."

"Does she live in England?"

"Yes."

"She will be safe there."

He wanted to stop the car, just hammer the footbrake and stop it; and embrace her, because she was a woman and she understood; because, in a strange car with a foreigner, all the maternity of a woman could not be concealed. Amidst the rising wreckage of her own life, she felt a damn site more than polite curiosity for a fifteen year old who, at this moment, would be out in Derby, in a discotheque or some such; and her mother would be at home, in the narrow living room, cramped by the piano, against one wall, which nobody ever played, and family photographs on the mantlepiece, watching the bequeathed grandfather clock until the fifteen year old returned.

Wurmstrasse, and Clark saw the cluster of street signs, some qellow, some blue, the blue for the autobahns. Garmisch-Partenkirchen was directly ahead and he followed, the traffic slowing now, faltering into the snow. A kilometre away, more signs. Garmisch-P. left. They were on a fly-over, a curve on stilts with a dual carriageway below. Down there, Clark could see other cars, cramped, static, their windscreen wipers moving in unison, the unknown, bored faces behind them, no more than shadows.

Tram lines further on, and the traffic released them. Walfriedhofstrasse, and a tram passed, carrying a handful of people in the three carriages, faces against the window. The driver in the cabin was young and hatless, holding the lever which made the tram go forward.

Then the cross-roads, the Dresdner Bank, and the cemetery. Snow clung to the branches of the trees. A furtive man was emerging from the wrought-iron gates, head bowed, his neck too thin for the collar of the shirt, the skin of the throat tightened and furrowed.

They turned left again, onto the autobahn, running alongside the cemetery.

"I saw the papers," the girl said. "Arthur showed them to me. I lied about that to your friend. Please don't tell him." They were doing a steady 100kph, following an Austrian heavy lorry which was churning snow from its rear wheels like sea spray. "You won't beat me for telling you?"

They reached the end of the cemetery. A landscaped area gave onto private houses. They were on the autobahnkreuz, and the sign said: Munchen-Furstenried. But was only to a southern suburb, and Clark ignored it. A chemical factory rose, prehensile, by the road, smoke filtering from three chimneys; and behind it, a wide, deserted office-block.

"I saw the papers." She repeated it for a reason which Clark could not comprehend. He was overtaking the lorry, in the fast lane, and already the cars were building up behind him, impatient to be past. "But you know all about them." She said it precisely because she sensed he didn't: The female intuition, applied to the practical.

"They don't always tell us everything, not in this line of business." He had to admit that. She was so young, perhaps twenty, and now she, like Klaus, had this power over him, the power of a little knowledge he had been deliberately denied.

He pulled back into the slow lane, in front of the lorry; and the cars were overtaking, like a flight. Suitcases and small pieces of furniture were strapped to roof-racks and protected by sheets of clear polythene which flapped at the unsecured corners and edges. "You tell me." He abaised himself in the request. Major Clark, brought to this; Major Clark who commanded absolute obedience from hardened soldiers and, over the years, had required a dignity of position which, within the wire mesh of a military camp, was never questioned. "I tried to protect you at the cemetery." The verbal gesture, inescapably necessary.

She could have been lying. She had lied to Klaus. She had admitted as much. But. . . .

"He copied them. They weren't originals," she said. "At first, I thought it was some joke. Lists of numbers. He said they were names and details. Some in Denmark, some in Norway; a few in Holland. Most in West Germany itself."

"And England.?"

"He didn't mention that." She, too, hesitated. They were in open country. The suburbs had fallen away, and the traffic was heavy, both carriageways full, nose to tail. "I had to ask Arthur what it all meant. He was very casual about it at first.

'Nothing, really,' he said. 'Nothing to get excited about.' We were in a cafe in Munich, eating gateau. It was in the afternoon. The cafe was full of those fashionable women who seem to spend their time in places like that. They must have rich husbands or rich lovers. Unlike me."

"What names?"

"People's names. And after each name, some information I didn't understand, either. It was in code, a mixture of numbers and letters and funny little symbols. 'Arthur,' I said, 'what good is all this? Why should we run away just because of some numbers?' He said the names and numbers were very important and worth a lot of money. He wouldn't tell me what they meant. I asked several times. It was my life as well as his. I was an accomplice, or whatever a court of law would call it. He could put on a sad face, could Arthur, like a beaten dog. That was what he did then. He took his spectacles off and wiped them very slowly with his handkerchief. He let me look into his eyes. They seemed to be sunk back deep into his head. 'I can't tell you,' he said. But he spoke with his eyes, you see. And they said: Please do not ask this question again."

The suitcase was rocking against the back seat, in unison with the rhythm of the car. The label was on the far side, unseen.

"He told me a little more later. He's so patient, you see. There are no contradictions in him. He can wait for anything, for a day or a week . . . or a year."

"Or four years."

She nodded; he caught the gesture; she caught the intonation.

"What did he tell you?" It was the direct question, and Clark was demanding an answer.

"I shouldn't reveal this," she said. "The names were real people, but, working in an office in Brussels, he couldn't even be sure of that. So he selected a name and activated the procedure. It was somebody in Coburg. That's north of Munich. Nobody would ever have heard of the place, but Hitler had a rally there early on, and somebody was killed. The Nazis made him into a martyr and had some repellent ceremony each year to mark the occasion. They would have done, wouldn't they?"

"Activated what?"

"I've told you."

"No, I mean the details."

"He sent off a telex, using the code. He had the current code-words, changing from day to day, he had everything. It worked. The same afternoon, the telex queries started coming back. The man wanted to know why he had been activated and — he used angry phrases — what he was supposed to do now. Arthur was very pleased. He telephoned me and told me to prepare to leave. Just one suitcase, he said. That suitcase. We met at Aachen. I was living there, working as as secretary. It's strange you and your friend never asked me about that. Your friend wanted to know about everything else. Arthur was in the Volkswagen, and we drove to Munich. It took the whole night because the Volkswagen doesn't go very quickly and Arthur can't see well in the dark. He wears special spectacles, you know, because he's short sighted."

"I know."

"But he is determined. He kept on driving, even when I could see how tired he was, the same 70kph. Even the lorries were going quicker than we were."

Pine trees ran up to the autobahn at both sides, the silent, uncharted forests of the night.

They drifted past a raststop, and a long queue of cars were waiting for petrol. They drove in silence for a long time. Clark was thinking about Klaus, alone in the flat; at the window, watching the snow, his feet naked because the ankle would remain swoollen; waiting, not as Dahlem would have waited, drawn back into himself, but assertive, hostile and impatient.

"What was the man supposed to do — the man he activated?"

"I don't know. I only know it happened. By this time I wasn't curious anymore. If you want the truth, I was very frightened."

The tanks will come. He sensed it. He thought of the Dane. He wondered if he had a ticket for London, an open ticket, valid for any airline. Gorlish would. The others would, too. Maybe the Dane would stay, would melt away, disguised as a country parson. The instinct for underground survival would be there, an unconscious skill, like riding a bicycle, even after thirty years. Clark pictured again the trimmed, neat figure poised behind the desk, the cultured hands like tentacles round the blotting pad, the eyes restless. The Dane would stay. Klaus wouldn't. Klaus would jump a train, hitch a lift. Klaus would hold the knife under somebody's chin and make them drive him. But Klaus would go.

"How many names were there on the papers?"

"I never counted them. But there seemed a lot. Well over a hundred."

The autobahn ended when they were thirteen kilometres from Garmisch, narrowed and curved to the left, back onto the old road, the snow beginning to bank in the hedgerows. The cars were solid in front of them, a procession of red tail lights following, slowly, the contours of the road. Ski country, and hoardings and placards along the verge, proclaiming the virtues of this hotel and that; pointing towards ski lifts and chair lifts, and a health hospital with salt baths. Ten o'clock, and they could see the week-end chalets now, fashioned of planks and logs and painted livid colours; quaint as Swiss cuckoo-clocks.

"The Brenner has been closed for a week," Clark observed. The procession halted short of Garmisch itself and they waited, in the country, the railway line alongside the road and a signal in the stop position. "Maybe we won't get through here." An American military lorry was coming towards them, the canvas rear closed, the headlights full on. A jeep followed it. "How old are you?"

"Twenty two."

They moved off, thirty or forty yards, stopped again. The car in front was full of children clambering across the back seat. From time to time, the driver turned to still them but it was no good: The children couldn't bear the constriction. He thought again of Klaus.

They moved once more, another forty yards. The sign said: Garmisch 3km.

The procession would be going right through and on, up the mountainside, to the frontier. It could take the whole night; like Dahlem, and the Munich run. The whole bloody night.

"Twenty two is very young," Clark said.

"Very young for what?"

He felt gauche. She was two decades younger than he, and seperated by eternity itself; but she could still have been a mother of three at that age. Easily.

The other carriageway was empty and the snow lay upon it like a carpet. Only the wide tracks of the American lorry remained and the narrower ones of the jeep, equidistant grooves. The snow was already filling them.

"Dahlem is a criminal," Clark said. "A common law thief, apart from the damage he could do."

She did not reply to this.

Forty five minutes later, they limped into Garmisch and reached an intersection with a traffic island in the middle of it and a policeman directing the columns of cars. They turned south, towards Mittenwald. That was twelve kilometres away; three more after that to Schnartiz and the frontier. They climbed and the snow stopped. The Alps were spread before them. Very suddenly, the night was clear, the rim of stars along the Milky Way like an arc of incandescent dust; the greying mountain peaks strained up at them; and the crevices and gullies below, like long slits, were choked with fallen rock and solitary pinetrees, the roots trailing across the stoneface, seeking a little soil. It was deathly quiet, except for the subdued murmur of motor engines before and after them, waiting to move forward again; it was a night for lovers to stroll, making snowballs; a night to breathe the chilled, pure, cleansing air and regard the stars in awe and wonder.

It was no kind of a night to be with a frightened girl, struggling towards Innsbruck to meet a man who was crazy.

Klaus was asleep in the chair when he heard the noise. At first he thought it was somebody trying to get into the flat; but he had placed an empty lemonade bottle behind the door, and they would have had to knock that over first. In fact the noise was coming from below. He listened, dissecting the merged voices: three youths, looters or burglars or drunk. A woman's voice joined them, at a different pitch, charged with apprehension and indignation, telling them to go away. They must have pushed her aside. Furniture was being shifted around. He heard obscenities, the taunting, mouthed, thoughtless obscenities of youth. The woman screamed but that was useless. The police were fully occupied elsewhere. The neighbours were behind locked doors, pretending not to hear; better to offer help when the youths had gone; to emerge diffidently, commisserate, and help clear up the mess. . . .

They came out and mounted the stairs, careless of the noise they made. The alcohol and the absence of police gave them an irresistable immunity.

The knife was in the bedroom, on the side table, and he had gathered it up when the first boot struck the door. Another boot, higher up, muffled giggling; a third boot. Perhaps they had taken turns. Klaus thought the lock would burst. He opened the door and it knocked the bottle over, sent it rolling in a wide circle past him. He had been right. Three of them, aged sixteen or seventeen, with T-shirts under their overcoats. One, nervous and uncertain, had positioned himself at the back. He was so young he hadn't even begun to shave. Wisps of dark hair, flecks not yet strong enough to be stubble, covered his chin and throat. He was drawn between needing to flee and lacking the courage to do it.

They all saw the knife, as if it had a brutal, hypnotic fascination.

"We want a drink." The eldest spoke. They laughed, forcing it because they were in the wrong and no amount of alcohol could re-shape them, no amount of immunity could alter their ethics.

Klaus just smiled: The slow, rolling smile with the lips close together.

"Come in and get one," he said quietly.

Nobody moved. Their eyes were still on the knife, on the chip in the blade, making it into a ragged saw which would tear the flesh as it penetrated; on the polished wooden haft locked in a strong hand, the point of the blade low and aimed upward, just as it had been against Clark, inside the wrought iron cemetary gates.

"You kicked the door," Klaus said. He motioned casually towards it with the blade of the knife. The door might have been an exhibit for the prosecution in a dry courtroom, wreathed in silence.

"An accident." Prudence before bravado. "I slipped and fell." He tried to make it into a joke to impress his comrades; but they weren't laughing now. They were edgy. He'd seen that before, Klaus had; it gave him no pleasure. It was just a fact of his life, whenever he smiled like that and held the blade low, his arm a lever so that the blade came up at an angle and none could escape it.

"Twenty marks to repair the door. You give me twenty

marks."

They turned and ran. He heard their scattered footfalls on the stairs, the echoes of the rush across the courtyard; heard the oaken door pulled frantically back as they struggled to gain the street. Then he walked down the stairs himself, in his bare feet, the concrete cold against them, and knocked once with his closed knuckles at the door of the flat below. The woman shuffled behind it but would not open it.

"I live upstairs," Klaus said.

"Go away."

"You ever see them before?"

"No." Her face must have been close to the door on the inside. "They were going to steal things but they were too drunk. They drank some wine and spread the rest over the carpet. They broke china which my grandmother gave me. Real Dresden china, pre-war. Three figurines. I nearly wept when they did that. I don't care about the carpet."

"Relax," Klaus said. "They're gone now. They won't come back." He walked slowly back up the stairs. The teenagers weren't even looters. That would come next. They were just tasting a little anarchy.

Klaus had imagined that the people from the east had set them up to it, feeling him out. Jesus, he could have laughed himself, now. The people from the east should be so stupid. He'd killed a man in Wiesbaden eighteen months ago. Cut the tendons of his throat. That must have been on their files. At least, he hoped it was. A man was entitled to some recognition.

So what did they think he would do to a few kids in T-shirts?

He put the kettle on again.

They sat in the car. It had become a cell; the view from the windows was wonderful but there was no leaving and no choice of inmates. Solitary confinement is not available.

"Your daughter," the girl wondered. It was the outcrop of some subterranean current of thought. "Is she beautiful? Perhaps I can meet her one day, if ..."

Clark grunted something. That was the worst being English. Kindness, even in small measures, made him vulnerable.

Mittenwald: A cluster of chalets grouped at the base of the mountains, the lights from the windows beacons in the dark. Sheep grazed in the meadow beyond, not needing sleep. An old timber tavern leant out over the road, the metal sign above the door motionless; there was no wind.

The tavern was closed, the shutters bolted, the bare shrubs in the flower-bed along its front covered in snow. Clark opened the car door to look ahead. The procession was as far as he could see, on the road weaving through the village and up again, up into the mountains. A few minutes later they crept over a wooden bridge and halted on the far side of it. The water was running fast beneath them, gurgling and choking over smooth stones.

Midnight. He switched on the radio. AFN. The American Secretary of State had arrived in Moscow for urgent talks. NATO reconnaisance planes were reporting that tanks in the east were being grouped into formations, though the pattern of them was not yet established. A MIG fighter had violated the Allied air corridor to West Berlin, north of Magdeburg, and had buzzed a Dutch scheduled flight, ordering it — over the intercom and in English — to turn back. But reports about that were confused. The KLM pilot, Johannes something or other, was not available for comment. The British government had condemned the escalation of tension in the strongest terms at the United Nations, in New York; but the motion, to have an immediate conference on the maintenance of peace in Europe, had been defeated by the bloc African vote.

The girl made no comment.

"The Africans. . . ." Clark said. "What the hell do they know about it?"

"You're a racialist," she said. "I wouldn't have expected that."

They waited beyond the bridge for half an hour, on an incline. Clark turned the engine off. Forty minutes. Fifty minutes. A snow-plough came past them, the chains on its tyres grating against the surface of the road. Then they moved on up for two kilometres, stopped again. The drivers in front were getting out and walking up the road. Clark said: "I'll be back in a minute," Outside the car, he inhaled deeply and felt the air sting the back of his throat. He was almost breathless.

He followed the other drivers a long kilometre in the cleared snow, in the margin which the snowplough had brushed away. Over the spur of a hillock, he saw the frontier: A brick building at the roadside, supporting a plastic canopy which stretched across the width of the road. A red and white pole, on a pivot, had been positioned under it, to be raised by a hand winch to let vehicles through. Two Austrian customs officials in blue uniforms faced the growing crowd.

And the crowd will always produce a spokesman; a man who emerges. He may be a barrack-room lawyer or a fool; his motives are uncertain; but the moment for expressing the collective impulse is his, and he takes it, savours it, sometimes with great self-righteousness, sometimes with great humility, because he knows that he is the spokesman, appointed without a vote, and no other will come forward.

He was a tall figure, lean, even in an overcoat buttoned up to the throat, with the smooth, outmoded, short hair of a fanatic straight across the back of his head. He stood away from the crowd, as if to emphasise his importance; stood nearer the customs officials, who were at each end of the red and white pole. And the crowd edged nearer to him, the anonymous strength of numbers.

He was a heckler, gesticulating with both hands; an orator, communicating in the sublime with his captive audience because he expressed what they wished to be expressed and wouldnot do it themselves.

"Closed," he cried out, equally, to the two men in front and the many behind. "You have no right to close the frontier, no right!" The muted murmur of agreement travelled back; the meek assertion of precisely that strength of numbers. "You've taken our money before and now you want to turn us away like orphans! Austria couldn't have survived for a day — a single day — without good German money!" He turned, seeking further confirmation: The mute mandate to go on. The crowd drew closer, almost joining him, unafraid of being associated with him now.

"We financed you like a protectorate! We gave you. . . ." and he opened his arms, embracing the land beyond the mountains, ". . . we gave you everything. Factories, loans, credits. You were Nazis once, when it suited you, and then you went neutral. You didn't want the guilt. We didn't even insist on your guilt. We allowed you to re-write your history for all your little children — they must never know what daddy was really like. We let you forget — we let you yodel in the mountains and let the cow bells lull you to sleep." Laughter rose. "My friends, it is not the time for cheap humour." They fell silent at the rebuke; the spokesman knew best. He must be obeyed. He took a step nearer the pole, as if it was something symbolic which must be faced. "The Austrians didn't want to work like Germans. That offended you, the work, you wanted to sit on the mountainside and take German marks from German tourists while we re-built. We re-built you out of our pocket-money!" Neither of the officials had moved. They stood like sentries, hands behind their backs, their capes draped over their shoulders, baggy at the knees, tri-angular silhouettes.

A voice from deep within the crowd — deep and safe —

called out: "Yes, and they stole from me. The police stole from me. They fined me for speeding and they wouldn't even let me defend myself, down in Steiermark last summer. A roadside fine, they called it. I'd been following an Austrian car, but they didn't stop him — they waved him through!"

The movement forward had begun.

The official on the right saw and sensed it at the same moment; groped beneath his cape and let them all see the black, leather revolved holster at his waist.

"Smash the pole." It came from no single person; it was a tribal chant; an expediency which had suddenly become a great truth. They surged. Clark was at the back, his view obscured and fragmentary. He saw hands seize the pole and drag it backwards, ignoring the winch, until the wood snapped; saw it raised, shoulder high, and cast down, the broken end ragged, into the gutter.

Some drivers were already running past him, back down the incline, towards their cars. They just wanted to get through. Clark remained for a moment. One official had gone; had run into the snow; two Germans had seized the other, dragged him away so that he would not obstruct the traffic, and were beating him. His peaked cap had fallen into the snow and lay upturned. A foot went into the man's rib-cage, like a punch delivered at short-range. More Germans were in the brick building, ransacking it in impotent rage. The telephone wires were torn from the breeze blocks in the wall. Assistance could not be summoned now.

As Clark turned, he scanned the faces of those who remained, scattered about him, the helpless bystanders; scanned, too, the knot which had gathered around the two men still beating the official. The first of the cars was coming up, others following, on the wrong side of the road to avoid the cars still parked. One had a chair on a roof-rack, and he wondered why they had chosen to salvage that.

He walked to the car. The girl sat precisely in the position where he had left her, her eyes half-closed, her legs crossed, indifferent to what might have been happening.

"We can go through," Clark announced. "They are destroying the frontier."

"Who is?"

"The Germans. Nothing will stop them from getting over into neutrality. They almost killed one of the frontier officials. Perhaps they have by now."

She opened her eyes wide, as if to fend off sleep.

"I had a good look at the ones who weren't brave enough to join in. I had a good look at the spectators." He paused. He was uncertain how to say it; but he needed to say it. "They were enjoying it." Not a Jew, not a Russian, not a simple Communist, even; just a stupid Austrian official, speaking the same language, shaped by the same culture, obeying his instructions. "They were enjoying it." He repeated the sentence, as if he could never reconcile the revelation.

"Were you brave enough to join in?" She did look at him. Her face was illuminated by the snow up the hillside beyond her. And then, because he would not reply: "What would you do if your daughter was in this car? Turn back — or go through?"

For the first time, he hated, her, too.

They reached Innsbruck at four in the morning. The town was full of cars with German registration plates. There had been no fresh snow here; the old lay in frosted, soiled heaps on the pavements. Clark found the railway station, a long, low ugly building fashioned of concrete and closed up for the night, long ago. A single taxi was in the rank in front of it, the driver asleep at the wheel. The hotel was on the corner opposite. He was too tired to care about anything else. The girl had drifted into sleep before Seefeld; had gone limp and fallen slowly forward so that he had had to reach out an arm and draw her back into her seat. Now, as he parked by the hotel, on the corner, she murmured and partially opened her eyes. She was still held in the grip of a dream. She looked round as if the shapes before her were from the unreal world.

They went into a spacious entrance hall. The porter sat submerged behind a desk at the far end of it, reading a newspaper. A cigarette burned in the ashtray on the counter where he had placed it; a narrow thing, rolled by himself with small strands of tobacco straggling.

"My name is Clark." He had no idea what to do if they had let the room to someone else. It was too late, and he couldn't face a night in the car. "You have a room for me, a double room with single beds. Two single beds." The porter traced an old finger down the ledger, found the name and the room number enscribed against it. Herr Clark. He looked up at the girl. He must have been wondering why they weren't in a double bed. She couldn't have been his daughter. . . .

The porter said: "Room 47. Fourth floor." He swivelled in the chair, took the key from the rack and slid it across the counter. "The lift is over there." Clark had expected him to take the girl's suitcase up, but he was already back into the newspaper. The cigarette had gone out, leaving a horn of cold ash.

As they walked towards the lift, the porter looked up and said pointedly: "You're lucky. A hundred Germans have asked for that room tonight. They offered to pay double and treble the rate, some of them. It was kept for you because this is a very respectable hotel." Whether that was an insinuation about Clark sharing a room with the girl was not clear. They were in single beds, after all. "And you're British, too. Not like the Germans. Between us, it is a matter of honour." He wore a pocket watch, the silver chain hanging from the button hole of the lapel. He took it out and cradled it in the palm of his hand. "Thirteen minutes past four," he said. "Not many hotels in London would have kept a room so long."

SUNDAY

She had formally requested Clark not to touch her during the night. That had been a difficult moment. She had insisted on undressing in the dark after threatening to get into bed fully clothed, if that was necessary. He resented this. "I trust you, of course," she had said, her weary eyes drifting around the room as if it were a transit camp. She didn't bother to unpack. "I don't know why but I do. It's something in your manner. But I only ever trust a stranger so far . . ."

They woke at nine. The dressing was awkward, too, and Clark went into the bathroom to do it; emerged and said: "I'll wait for you downstairs, in the breakfast room."

They sat all morning in the lounge, a high, pretentious room, wide and vast, scattered with sofas and arm chairs, and perodicals, mostly German, in a heap on a mahogany table. The reception desk was through opened double doors, the restaurant through more, in the other direction. The room was full of Germans, disciplining their children and talking of staying until the crisis was over. "We've taken our room for a whole month," a woman near them confided," "just to be sure. My husband has had to give up his job." Elsewhere, they discussed the exchange rate at the railway station and the fluctuations in it, so that different people were able to parade their acumen — or their luck — in changing marks at just the right time. The fluctuations were happening hourly now. And the KLM plane hadn't done the rate any good at all.

A party of Austrian schoolchildren waited for a bus outside the station, holding skis and helmets: The undisturbed normality.

The call came at exactly twelve o'clock. "Frauline Ingermann." It was a voice over the tannoy, flat and slightly indistinct. "Telephone for Frauline Ingermann. Please come to the reception desk."

They went there together and were directed into a booth, one of three set against a wall. She lifted the receiver and said simply: "Ingermann." The booth smelt of human sweat, stale and still pungent; it was mixed with lingering perfume.

"Yes," she said, "Yes, I am here, I am waiting for you. It was so long in the night, travelling, worse even than going to Munich; but I am safe. Are you?" Clark was behind her, and he could not prevent his body brushing against hers. The booth was too small. He craned forward, ungainly, trying to hear. "I love you. Nothing has changed. I love you. Yes, I will wait." She held the receiver in her hand for an instant when the conservation was over, reluctant to replace it and sever the cord which had joined them.

When they came out, he thought she was going to cry. "I can't bear to think of those people hunting him like an animal," she said. The receptionist was looking at them with great curiosity: Two people in a booth. They sat again, in the same seats, as if by habit; remained for a long time. "He senses that I am not here alone," she said. "I could have told him and you would never have known. I could have spoken spoken the words in German slang which you can't understand; but he sensed it anyway. He's always been like that. The infirmity heightened his perception. I wonder if that is on his medical card, too."

Clark said: "We should go and have some lunch. There must be restaurants nearby. I fancy a walk. I don't see the necessity to sit here, hour after hour." She nodded distantly. Her thoughts were far away, on the man wearing spectacles.

They wandered towards the centre of the town. Clark couldn't be sure, because this was Sunday and a great many people were on the streets strolling. He couldn't be sure because he'd been trained in military intelligence and pedestrians didn't wear insignias on their shoulders, or cap badges; they didn't carry rifles whose distinctive shapes betrayed their marques; but they weren't being followed.

Klaus took the call from the Dane at three. He listened, making no observation. Then he telephoned for a taxi. A taxi at six. He thought he'd better book it early.

He was at the window at five-thirty. A little snow lay on the planks of the windows opposite, shaded now from the low sun which hung somewhere beyond the cloud. He saw the taxi come, a Mercedes, probing, slow and uncertain, for number 101; went down to it. He had no key for the flat door. The girl had neglected to leave him that. Too bad.

The driver talked constantly. "They're driving like mad people," he said. It was a hazard which means a great deal to him. "They're jumping the lights. There was a big fight in the Viktualienmarkt last night. Women. They panic first. Where do you want to go?"

"Waldfriedhof."

"The churches were full this morning. You know the Protestant place over at Pasing? There was a queue outside it right round the block. They had some kind of open air service for them because they couldn't get them all in, even standing. A matinee performance." He shook his head in bewilderment before this knowledge. A van veered towards them, and he manipulated the wheel, taking the Mercedes towards the kerb and out of the way. "Madness," he said bitterly. "A few drunken reporters start writing stupid stories and everybody goes off their heads. So a few tanks get moved about in the east. They get bored over there and they think: Let's move the tanks around. And everybody goes crazy. I've been to the airport five times today, three this morning. The hall out there is like that church — so full they can't get any more in. I've never seen so much luggage. I took an old woman out. She tried to get her whole house into the taxi. 'Listen,' I said, 'there's no room for all that. They won't let you put all that on a plane. It would never get off the ground!' You know what she did? She made me pull off the road into a lay-by at Daglfing and she started just throwing the stuff out of the taxi. So we get to the airport. A shambles. Those people, they'll go anywhere. Lisbon, Morocco, South Korea, Taiwan, Detroit. Anywhere. I saw a woman at the ticket counter with a kid. They were both crying. Imagine that."

The cemetery: Dahlem had one of those minds, moving in regular circles.

Klaus paid the taxi driver by the tram terminus and walked quickly towards the wrought iron gates. The wind was skimming the snow beneath his feet. He checked the time: 6.21. He was nine minutes early.

He found the pond.

Why did Dahlem want to do it this way? Maybe he would just hand across the papers, but it was no guarantee the girl would be freed. Of course, the Dane had promised she would be. But nobody could be stupid enough to believe that. Klaus scuffed the gravel impatiently, like a restless horse. Maybe Dahlem did trust the Dane. It was always possible. The Dane was certainly the kind you might trust, if you were innocent enough. The father figure. Dahlem's own father had died.

The Dane had even told Dahlem that the hour was late — what a flowery phrase, pompous and semi-Biblical — and he was only interested in the papers. No charge would be brought for taking them. He'd avoided the word steal; it was, he felt, too emotive.

Klaus would accept the papers; Klaus would telephone Baden Baden to give the assurance that he had them; and the Dane would telephone Innsbruck. A daisy-chain. Dahlem

could make his own way, unhindered, to Austria and simply
go away with the girl; go to that lakeside he wanted, buy an
axe, and start work on the log cabin.

6.27.

Klaus leant back and twisted the brass tap, tightening it, to
stop the dripping; the washer had worn away and he could
only make it drip more slowly. He turned back. An old
woman all in black knelt at a distant grave, her knees in the
snow, murmuring. The cadence of it, the metre of each line,
reached him. She had her hands pressed together, her head
bowed into her neck, like a sleeping crow. She wore a lace
shawl which she had arranged around herself in a head-scarf.

She remained until the toll from the church marked 6.30.

She walked towards him without seeming to notice him.
Came to him, in short, spasmodic shuffles, saw him, smiled;
some teeth were missing and, suddenly, she looked an old
hag.

"Water," she said. "Will you carry some back, please? It's
too heavy for me."

He was undecided; finally nodded. He walked the three or
four paces to the metal stand, lifted a can and returned to the
pond. He sat on the brick wall and stretched for the tap, to
turn it on. She stood away, the old fingers of each hand
interlocked, like the branches above.

He saw the face in the water: A distorted face, fluid and
without proportions, the eyes enlarged, the water a mirror
which revealed and concealed. He saw the shoulders, wide,
seeming to reach up to the head itself as if there was no neck.
He saw the whole move at him, an arm raised.

He knew there would be no shooting. Other people would
be in the cemetery. It was Sunday night. It would have been
better to shoot him as he walked in; shoot from a car.

His hands were at his head as he turned.

The first blow was a rabbit-punch to his neck. The collar of
the flying jacket partly cushioned that. The second was a

boot which struck his thigh.

He punched at something.

He saw them: A heavy man in a raincoat with strong hands, another, behind him, taller, blond hair flapping.

He had no time to reach for the knife. He felt the hands grasp the lapel of the flying jacket, jerking him forward; felt the knee in his groin; felt the hands force him backwards towards the pond, and the brick wall hit at the back of his knees.

His teeth were clenched.

He butted the man who held him, the head lowered like a bull, the crown of it — a piston. The impact made him feel sick; but the hands were released, and he had the knife, and he pressed it into the belly of the raincoat as hard as he could. It sliced through the fabric, resisted when it reached the lowest rib of rib-the cage. He leant on the handle, twisted it, and the man fell away from him.

There was blood on the blade.

Clever little Dahlem. Clever boy. Wouldn't Mummy be proud. He didn't come personally. Oh no. He rang up the people from the east and invited them to come instead.

Klaus surveyed the tall man. "Don't try and bring anything out of your pockets," he said. "I might not like that." The woman had gone. "You know what we're going to do? We're going to stand here and watch him die. That shouldn't take long. Forty minutes, fifty minutes". Klaus looked down. The man in the raincoat had closed his eyes. His arms were limp in the snow. His legs were tucked in and folded double, like a jack-knife. The blood must have been seeping from the incision, but it was still within the raincoat. The cut in the coat was very small, a narrow slit, no more than a tear by a bramble bush. "I could make it quicker if I wanted to, but I don't. If people come wandering by . . ." and he shrugged his shoulders to indicate circumstances beyond his control. He wiped the blade of the knife on his trouser leg.

"We're very hygenic on our side of the fence," he said. "How much did you pay the woman?" The tall man was motionless. He might have been thirty five; around that. He wore black, fur snow boots, zipped at the sides. "If you put your hands near your pockets, I'll cut your throat. Just twitch and see what happens."

A minute of silence. Both men were calculating. Both men understood that.

"How much did you pay the woman?"

"Enough." The voice was thin and almost effeminate. A pansy, an intellectual, probably, who abhorred violence. The commissar to supervise the thug. Like Clark. He hadn't even tried to join in when the other man held Klaus.

But Klaus had to tell the Dane. Klaus had to make a call. Dahlem would be on his way to Innsbruck now, on the evening train, reading a cheap paperback and looking self-satisfied. The papers would be in his pocket, unless he'd flushed them down the toilet and just let them billow away, the wind carrying them from the railway line across the fields.

The man on the ground tried to say something. The wind dragged the snow over one of his hands and it began to fill the gaps between the fingers. He closed the hand, a reflex action, the muscles and nerves responding instinctively. Like an electric shock. Then he turned his whole body in a slow roll, the head limp, and Klaus could see the blood coming through the slit in the raincoat.

"Some questions," Klaus said. "Lots of questions." His groin hurt abominably from the boot and he half-stooped. He couldn't stop himself.

The man pushed at him — not even a punch, but a push and Klaus was off-balance.

He ran. His feet scattered snow and gravel as he went. He lengthened his stride, his coat billowing behind him, reached the end of the avenue and was gone.

Klaus was against the pond wall. The pain was worse.

After a long interval, the bell tolled seven.

He walked uncertainly back to the gates, crossed to the terminus and searched for a telephone box; found one, a metal cubicle, alone on the pavement. He rang Baden Baden first, on a collect call, and spoke briefly to the Dane. Then he rang the emergency services. "An ambulance, please," he said. "A man in the cemetery at Waldfriedhof. You can't miss him. He's by the pond, in avenue fourteen. He says he's got very bad stomach ache."

Clark and the girl sat in the hotel lounge. They had eaten in an Italian restaurant, but that was only a memory. The Dane had rung. Now it was dusk, and cocktails were being served — a legacy from the English era when a £ sterling was worth 70 schillings, not a miserable, impoverished 20-odd, and the mountains were thick with colonels and city people on wooden skis, taking the air.

The television had been switched to ZDF, the German channel. That was better for news programmes. If you only wanted old American films, it didn't matter. Any Austrian channel was as good.

Seven-fifteen, and the scheduled programmes had been abandoned. A camera crew were on the roof of the airport outside Bonn, waiting for the American Forces plane. Another crew were camped in the arrival hall with the milling passengers moving carelessly in front of them, sometimes peering stupidly towards the camera and waving.

"We have checked with the airport radar," the presenter said, very gravely. "The plane is over Poland now, approaching Lodz. It is due to pass into East German air space in fifty minutes." The Moscow talks. Clark had almost forgotten.

Klaus rang for a taxi. He preferred to travel in them for no reasons of security; they flattered his vanity, especially since he wasn't spending his own money. The number was engaged. The wind stirred again, as if the buildings were funnelling it; it lifted the snow and fanned it against his legs. He closed the cubicle door. An unmanned tram had been left at the terminus, the snow gathering at its wheels. He dialled the number again. "There is a delay of several minutes," a girl said. "All taxis are engaged at this moment."

"I'll wait," he said. "I'm at the tram terminus at Waldfriedhof."

The ambulance came, the klaxon yearning, stopped by the cemetery gates. The back opened. Two attendants carried a stretcher in. Klaus walked up and down. Ice lay in a film over his toe-caps. They brought the man back, his body covered by a grey blanket, up over his head. They didn't do that for the wounded, only the dead. Then the police cars drew up, two of them, one at each end of the ambulance.

The taxi arrived. "Hauptbanhof," Klaus said.

The driver looked towards the cemetery gates.

"A drunk," Klaus said.

"Funny place to go when you're drunk," the driver said.

"Funny people," Klaus said. As he sat down, he felt the comforting shape of the knife against his thigh. The groin still hurt.

The streets were empty. Everybody was watching television, watching the camera on the rooftop probe into the night, waiting for the plane. Room lights filtered through drawn shutters, auras of white and yellow.

The demonstration was moving along the Miller-ring; a march timed, no doubt, to coincide with the television broadcast; to emphasise that some still cared. A few — the lost people, the curious people, the ordinary people, the bystanders — were on the pavement, waiting for it to pass. A heavy policeman stood in the middle of the road, at the intersection. He flagged down the taxi driver and told him to remain there.

Then they came, preceded by a police car, three abreast, the strands of feeling drawn together so that they were marching for many different things and precisely the same thing. Klaus surveyed the banners. Some had been used before, on other demonstrations; others had been created overnight, crude slogans daubed on sheets of bedding and secured to broom handles; and each, the new and the old, the echoless exhortations of the dreamers.

LIBERATION IS COMING! THE BOURGEOIS ARE FINISHED!
GERMANY WILL BE FREED TOMORROW!
WE ARE ALL GERMANS, EAST AND WEST!
VIETNAM IS ALL OUR GRAVES!
VOTE FOR STURM: PROGRESS THROUGH DISCUSSION!
THE YOUTH LEAGUE ARE ON THE MOVE!

And, at the very end, detached from the tramping people as if by deference to the occasion, a tramp holding a pole with a cardboard plaque on top of it, in multi-colours, advertising a night-club.

The bystanders cheered him, and he bowed his head in mock recognition, the old cove did, and bared his broken teeth. He was the only one who looked happy. The rest, some elderly, harbouring terrible rejections and brooding on political extremes, some young, students, brandishing the faith that all was possible, and the extremes really did make sense; they all looked crushed and miserable. There was no joy in the slogans but a kind of fatal exultation that the dreamers had always been right; and their time had come.

At the corner, right in front of the taxi, the trouble started. A bottle was thrown into the march and it broke them up. Four Bavarians were outside a chemist's shop, workmen in overalls, wanting a little excitement. "Why don't you run away?" one of them called out — a naked, graceless taunt.

"I'm surprised you're out in this weather. You could get a terrible chill."

The fight was between the pacifists who would fight and those who tramped, disconsolate, onward. The police were swarming. In the distance, Klaus heard the pump of a tear-gas bomb which fell short of the struggling groups. The smoke began to disperse, borne on the wind, towards them. A girl in jeans was caught by it and retched. She let her banner fall into the snow, and the wind plucked at it, as if it were a sail on high seas and a storm was coming. She covered her eyes. "Help me! Help me! It's the gas. The police are pigs . . ." One of the Bavarians held two bearded youths in a single, huge hand and beat aimlessly at them with his fist, their bodies jostling and rubbing against his. The police felled a man and he lay in the snow, blood on his forehead. He had no banner.

A woman was crying hysterically: "We've been betrayed." And then, detaching herself from the fighting: "The Americans will betray us, too!" She turned. Nobody but Klaus had noticed her. Nobody was listening. "Moscow . . ." she said.

"Delinquents," the taxi driver observed with distaste. "We're paying for them — and they behave like that. They ought to be in the army, the whole lot of them." The traffic policeman was no longer there. The driver eased the taxi forward, and they moved off.

At 7.36, the presenter was still talking; a smooth and polished and groomed man, middle-aged but guarding the secret of eternal youth, so that the mascara was visible — the discordant, unreal facial shades — when the camera moved directly onto him. The darkened relief brushed into his eyebrows to accentuate them blended in perfect harmony. The microphone was round his neck, on a cord, hanging half-way down the purple tie, so rich it was almost luminous. He faced the camera in the hall: Behind him, the crowd had grown, the aged, the ugly, the children, waiting obediently for flights, stepping across mounds of luggage and clutching coffee in plastic beakers. The human background had been arranged to capture the mood, a professional evaluation to enhance a television programme. That was what made Clark sick of it all — the evaluators. He wondered savagely if they would have an inquest on the production at ZDF, to see if it could be improved next time. He wondered if they would examine the audience ratings, at a meeting, with Tom and Dick and Harry there, each thrusting himself forward. He wondered if, just off camera, technicians were clinically checking the background light, the intrusion of noises, the level of sound — and a programme controller, with a sheaf of notes and ear-phones, was coldly monitoring the standard of production, breathing commandments to nervous secretaries.

But Clark was thinking about Heston. Ask any Englishman under thirty where it was, and they wouldn't have an idea. Heston: Disused now. It had been used then, when he was a child; used by Chamberlain who came back with a promise and a message and stood uncertainly before a microphone reading it, the wind pulling fitfully at the tails of his coat.

"It's all happening again."

He had forgotten who had spoken those words: The priest, Echtmann's girlfriend, the Dane. It didn't matter. They were true.

When the American landed, he was going to veil truth in optimistic noises. Everyone in the lounge sensed this. The question was: Could they penetrate the veil and see the truth for themselves?

"Do you think Dahlem will be watching?" Clark asked gently, because his relationship with the girl had now become gentle.

"I don't even know where he is," she said. "Perhaps there is no television set where he is." She had kept her coat on, although the room was warm; kept in on to be ready to leave, from moment to moment.

Just then, the presenter said that the plane had entered East German air space.

The Hauptbahnhof was a bare, functional railway station with a main concourse full of swarthy guest workers — that was the German description of them — who regarded it as a market place. The bureau de change, down a corridor, was closed. Ticket windows, mostly unmanned, were set into one wall. Beyond the barrier, the platforms were marked: Gleis eins, Gleis zwei . . .

The next Innsbruck train was 8.20.

Klaus had expected a repetition of the airport here; but it was all well-ordered. Trains don't evoke the same emotion. The platform was full of people. The guest workers ignored them and kept on talking, illustrating their conversation with Balkan gestures, the shoulders and arms acting in concert.

Thirty minutes to wait. He went to the self-service cafeteria, a dirty room with beer drinkers at the far end, away from the food, in a group. He bought a small bottle of distilled orange, placed it on a brown, plastic tray, took a straw and carried it to a table.

Three hours to Innsbruck. It was a slow train, stopping everywhere. Maybe he was too late. Maybe clever little Dahlem was already there.

Even the presenter was excited. The plane had come onto the radar screen near Marburg, a hundred kilometres away, as it wheeled in a southern sweep, banking, steadying, then approaching in a direct line. A murmur spread round the hotel lounge as the picture was transferred to the roof-top camera, which ranged like a telescope into the empty night sky, through the falling snow.

"It's shocking," a man near Clark said loudly. "They should have made the statement in Moscow before the

American left and prevented all this. Nothing is going to happen, anyway. A fool can see that. The mark is down seven pfennigs again today — all because of this charade."

"The Americans," somebody else said, just as loudly. "They always wait to see who's going to win before they declare war."

The girl inclined her head towards Clark. "You don't believe that, do you?"

He shook his head.

"Many times I think of this," she said. "I even asked Arthur, but he couldn't tell me. In the last war, the Hitler war, all the countries were on different sides. Now there are allies, except the Russians. How did this happen? And was it necessary for the thirty million to die, merely to rearrange geography in this fashion?"

Clark said: "What was in the papers Dahlem took?"

"I've told you: I never knew. I hope you don't think I tell lies."

"You told them to Klaus."

They had ordered coffee, and it arrived. A waiter in black trousers and white waistcoat, a diffident adolescent, laid the tray on the table and almost fawned for the tip. They were paying with marks, too. In some places in the town, nobody gave a damn about Austrian schillings. That was only play money, for ski holidays.

"There it is," and the presenter's voice was heightened and quickened. The camera craned uncertainly, finding nothing.

Klaus saw this, too. There was a television in the cafeteria, and it had silenced even the drinkers who had gathered beneath the shelf on which it stood.

A moment, a long, uneasy moment when the presenter sensed that it was no longer the time for commentary before the plane came into vision; and then they all saw the dimmed lights on the wing-tips; and, as they drew nearer, the carcas of the plane itself, dark in the darkness, obscured by the snow, a heavy, pig-like silhouette losing height as it descended. Suddenly it was low over the rim of pine-trees, boring down. The nose-cone tilted fractionally up and the wheels were feeling for the runway, moist where the underground heating had melted the snow. It was running forward, its speed slackened, into the lengthening shadow of the terminal building. The lettering United States Air Force was clear along the body behind the wing.

The disembarkation took only a brief while. The figure came out of the opened door in the flank of the plane, stooped involuntarily, waved with one hand to the three men who stood at the foot of the metal stairway, in a line, and came down. One of them shook the American's hand and they embraced, a bear-hug, arms wrapped around each other.

"They look like Russian comrades — or queers," a drunken voice in the cafeteria observed.

The black Mercedes was waiting, the pennant on the bonnet flapping in the wind. The figure waved again — he would know he was on television, he would expect that, being American — and was into it. Clark thought how difficult it was to get into a motor vehicle with dignity. He thought that because there were many other things he didn't want to think about.

The presenter, bereft of material, discussed solemnly the significance of the American waving twice. Then, confusion. They moved to the interview room but the camera showed nothing except an empty platform and ranks of journalists below it, on plastic seats.

Cameramen crowded round the platform, loaded like pit ponies with all their equipment harnessed to them.

Klaus had bent the straw by mistake, thrown it away and now pressed the bottle to his mouth to finish it. Ten minutes before the train left.

I hope you're watching this little lot, Dahlem, he thought. I hope there's a television in your little rabbit hole. I hope you're sitting comfortably. Then we'll begin.

The American came through a door at the back, preceded by the Mayor of Bonn. The door was made of the same orange hessian as the wall, and didn't look like a door at all until the instant it was opened. They sat at the table on the platform while the photographers swarmed around them, the flash bulbs igniting like some cosmic upheaval. The American looked tired. He was a young fifty, in a dark suit, with a curious face which was neither Saxon nor Slavonic nor Latin, but a blending. A mongrel, not a member of the master race. He put on his spectacles to shield his eyes from the flash bulbs.

"That's enough, boys," the Mayor said. He raised a hand. Still they continued. "If you don't stop, you will be required to leave . . ." The Mayor was a short man, wearing his chain of office; a man accustomed to obedience. But some of these photographers were foreign, not German . . .

The American had the statement on the desk in front of him. "I am authorised to make this statement by the State Department," he began. He adjusted his spectacles, craned nearer the microphones which were so sensitive that each breath, each pant, each inhalation was recorded.

Somewhere, out of sight, a translator had begun and half the reporters were putting on headsets to catch the German version.

"The Government of the United States of America has issued a strong protest to the Government of the Union of Soviet Socialist Republics concerning troop movements in central, northern and southern Europe. We recognise that such movements are not prohibited by either the SALT or Helsinki agreements signed freely by both governments; but we emphasise that such movements are against the spirit of these agreements. I am further authorised to say that the Government of the United States regards the entry of Soviet

military personnel into Finland with the gravest concern, and
has pointed out, during the talks in Moscow, that it can in no
way be justified except as an act aggressive in character and
intent. The Government of the United States notes with
displeasure that the President of Finland, a man freely elected
and one of the most respected political figures in Europe, is
now in Sweden and has officially applied for a resident's
permit. In our language, that means political asylum." He
looked up from the statement, surveyed the reporters. "I hope
you understand that, gentlemen." This had not been written
down, and was delivered more intimately, as an aside. He
resumed. "This statement is issued after full consultations
with all our allies." The after-thought.

A reporter in the middle of the room rose and tried to pose
a question.

The mayor, in English, said: "There will be no questions."

The American stood. Another reporter, towards the back
of the room, was yelling: "You call that a press conference?
You son of a bitch!"

But the American had gone back through the concealed
door, the Mayor following anxiously at his heels.

Klaus looked at the clock. He had four minutes, time
enough for a comfortable walk to platform seven.

"I bet the Russians are frightened of statements," someone
among the drinkers said. "They've sold us out. They've
traded us for a few words."

Clark was on his feet. Everybody else in the lounge was,
too, except the girl. Then the reaction, violent with the anger
of unreason.

"I wish the Fuehrer was here. He knew how to treat
Russians: Untermenschen!"

"The great ones were sacrificed: Rommell, von Runstedt,
Hoepner, Guderian. Their panzers would have protected us!"

"We should have brought my mother with us. I told you

she's not safe in Kassel, but you wouldn't listen."

An old woman, supporting herself by the arm of a chair, said: "I gave two sons in 1942." Nobody was listening. "Two honest boys, to comfort me in my old age. Dead. I don't even know where they're buried." The anger had seized her whole body, giving it sudden strength and impulse. "Why do the Germans always have to be punished?" She tried to struggle towards the television, as if she sought to attack it for defaming them. "Punish us," she went on, the dis-connected end of the sentence, "even when we're innocent."

The train was delayed indefinitely. Nobody was allowed to even board it. Klaus lay on a bench on the platform, on his side, One hand was against his groin, pressing it, soothing it with the warmth of his palm.

Every thirty minutes, a flat voice announced over the tannoy: "We regret the delay of the 20.00 hours train to Innsbruck. No further information is available.

Klaus knew. Any fool did. The Austrians had closed all the roads. The train crossing would be cut next. Then the airports.

In the event, the train left a handful of minutes before midnight.

MONDAY

It was full of guest workers, Turks and Yugoslavs and Greeks eating their raw, tinned fish and arguing. They were getting away. They'd come for the industrial harvest and now it was winter. The trees were bare. Time to go back to the dusty villages where old men play quoits and boules on the dried mud of the squares, and if you have a car, even an ancient British car, you're a candidate for president.

Greasy little people, Klaus thought. He was sitting by the window, watching the train pull away into the belt of factories which encircled Munich. Vagrants, unclean, with fat stomachs held in by soiled, synthetic trouser belts, and diminutive women at their sides. The men stank of oils and sweat, repugnant odours to any West European. They didn't shave and they didn't even clean their shoes.

He surveyed them, a whole carriage-full. The Americans are running away, why not you? Except the Americans will be going by aeroplanes in proper airlifts, refuelling at Greenland, and there will be reception committees to welcome them home, hospitality centres to accommodate them — but you, the real untermenschen, you'll find the Brenner has been closed this past week. Too bad you couldn't understand enough German to read the newspapers. The drain to the Balkans — the sewage pipe, is choked and severed. Another thing: Those German marks in your suitcases — they won't be worth one damn the moment the tanks move. Paper the walls with them, like my parents did.

Roll them into cigarettes, even notes of a hundred. Then stay and face it with us. You don't owe us that. It's just that, with the Brenner closed, there's nowhere to run. And if by any chance there is a seat on a plane, a seat on a train, a seat in a car, that will go to a German, not you. Nobody would permit creatures like you in their cars. You'd probably foul the seats.

The thoughts consoled him.

Sauerlach, a village; and the fields were stained with snow. Klaus noticed a barn with logs heaped against it, and the heads of the cattle within; and a cottage on the hillside, ablaze with light. The rhythm of the train dulled him by repetition. The Slavs were already asleep around him, their mouths grotesquely open, breathing heavily. The untermenschen could sleep anywhere, even on hard railway seats.

That's what we've lost, he reflected. It was curious. He had never been a man given to reflection, even though he had the degree. He'd gained that because he had a good memory.

That's what we've lost, and they have retained: The physical insensibility, like the Middle Ages.

He wondered absently when it would begin. Perhaps today.

Towards Rosenheim, at a point where the railway line curved towards the autobahn, he could see a military convoy heading north, the lorries equally spaced at regulation distance, headlights cutting into the night, the outriders leading in a phalanx of six motor bikes. The Bundeswehr. He couldn't see the soldiers in the lorries, but he knew enough about them: The juvenile conscripts, unfitted for jobs in industry, smoking furtively and peering out of the backs of the lorries, like the cattle.

Degerndorf, and the Alps were unfolding, pale and forbidding. The moon was up, its circumference perfectly defined, Berchtesgaden was the other way, on another railway line, further south, towards Salzburg. Too bad.

Chamberlain would have understood. It was a point of reference for the dead and the elderly, nothing more.

The frontier was still two stops away: Oberaudorf and Kiefersfelden. Innsbruck was five or six stops on the other side, if they got through. Another two and a half hours.

The man next to him, heavily asleep, drifted against him, let a limp arm fall across him. Klaus grasped the man's jacket and shook him. "Don't do that," Klaus said, as severely as if it had been a disguised homosexual attempt. "Don't you do that."

The man shifted his position to the other end of the seat, cupped both hands behind his head, fashioning a pillow, and went straight back to sleep.

Past Oberaudorf, Klaus went for a little stroll along the train, peering into the compartments. Most were asleep. American students had balanced ruck-sacks on the luggage rack, and these rocked uncertainly with the movement of the train. The waking ones seemed glazed. Their faces were turned to his in apprehension and curiosity.

If the people from the east were on the train, he couldn't pick them out. He really wanted the tall one, the sprinter, the man from the cemetery who had watched another die and made no move to help him; wanted to show him the knife again, wanted to make him answer all the questions.

Clark was awake. The girl lay in the other bed. At least she didn't snore. He wanted her. That was partly abstinence; of course. That was partly that she was there, four feet from him, twenty-two, innocent and unspoilt; available, in closer proximity than a barmaid; that was partly because he had seen her in the turmoil which he himself had known, and she had learned to accommodate it without sacrificing herself so that, in a very English way, he respected her.

He climbed out of the bed. She heard him, turned and looked at him.

"I was only going to the toilet," he said. He stood before her bed, wearing only pyjama bottoms.

"No," she said, reading the moment. If they had both been drinking, that might have altered everything; but they had not.

"I'm old enough to be your father," he said; a boy caught scaling the orchard wall.

Neither of them believed the implications of the excuse. That didn't matter. The answer was still no.

Klaus returned to his own carriage and stayed, standing, by the door. He had wound the window down and leant half forward, savouring the pure air and regarding the mountains which seemed to close on the railway line up ahead, as if the track had been cut into a gulley. Degerndorf, a quaint Alpine village with an old station and an old platform, illuminated by lights placed above hanging baskets of flowers. The train stopped. Whole families boarded it. They filled the corridors with their luggage; dispersed themselves, searching for unoccupied seats. As the train moved away again, labouring up the incline into the neck of the gully, and the pine trees had come to the base of the earthen platform on which the line had been laid, he was alone.

He felt somebody brushing past him and didn't even turn. It felt like a woman. He was wrong.

Two arms locked around his waist. His hands were on the chill, metal rim across the top of the lowered window, away from the knife. The arms had winded him. Another hand, a distant hand, reached for the chromium door-handle and opened it, in spite of the suction from the moving train; released it, so that it was flung back, hammering at the side of the carriage. Klaus was being driven towards the opened rectangle; the steps beneath the door, and the snow-covered slope, were running at him. His hands were on the wrists knotted in front of him, struggling to prise them open; thick wrists, scored by dark hairs.

The train was gathering speed.

He jerked his head back into the face of the man who held him. He sensed the impact, the head recoil.

It was too late.

He was tumbling down the incline, churning into the snow. He landed face down, but the momentum doubled him over and he could see the blue Alpine sky with great clarity as he somersaulted; spread his arms in front of him as he went down, the snow rising in plumes where his fingers gouged it. The pine trees were rushing at him and a protruding stone brushed his belly. His body rolled helplessly, turning him side-across the incline; he rolled once, twice, three times, and then he hit the tree trunk and he thought it had broken his back.

Clark went meekly back to sleep. The girl would never trust him again. The approach had destroyed the relationship built up over the two days. It could only make things more difficult now.

Klaus lay for a long time on his side. Degerndorf must be two or three kilometres back. He'd find a taxi there and make the driver go to Innsbruck.

He raised himself and leant against the trunk of the tree, one arm wrapped round the soft bark, looking back up the incline. His body had made the tracks of an upturning children's sledge as it came down; he could see the points where his feet had dug into the snow; the point where he had been twisted sideways, so that the smoothed area was now much wider; and, almost at his feet, the fallen pine cones which had been brushed away.

He hesitated, selecting his moment to try and walk, an indefinable moment when the mind and the body came together. He did begin to walk; almost stumbled and fell immediately; stopped where he stood, a hand reaching — probing delicately — for another tree trunk to grasp; hesitated again, more sure of himself; walked on, avoiding the stones. He reached a spur, and the valley spread before him, a thin road cut between the acres of pine trees. Far beyond them, where the pastures began, he could see the rooftops of Degerndorf.

Christ, he thought, that's a long, long way.

When he was out beyond the trees, on a muddied track, he started looking for a house. Any house with a telephone. Clark had to be informed that there were two of them, on the midnight train arriving at Innsbruck at God alone knew what hour. The customs might take an eternity. But when they got there, they'd take Clark apart. Just then, as he saw a light, further down, he remembered that Clark was totally unarmed.

Clark woke again at three. The girl — her eyes wide open — was watching him. The street lights had long been extinguished and the room was very dark, but he could see her eyes. The question of arms had been worrying him, too. He could hardly go out and buy a hand gun; he would be refused one. He could probably hire a hunting rifle, but what would they say in the hotel lounge if he laid it, telescopic sight and all, against a coffee table while he read the magazines? And he wasn't sure he would have been capable of using a gun, any gun, on a man, even if he had one. Better to venture nothing. Better to pretend that he had a military revolver under his armpit. What did they expect him to do: Empty six shots into the girl if she tried to run away?

He looked at her: Composed now, bearing a woman's suffering intuitively and without complaint or malice. It would be her life, and she had known this: To console the eunuch, to give him the tenderness, to face the rainy Tuesday afternoons when he would pace their little apartment thinking terrible, Satanic thoughts and she, perhaps, knitting in an arm-chair; would lay aside the ball of wool with infinite care and go to him and give him the simple faith to go on.

"Do you think Dahlem will be armed?" Clark asked.

"He's a pacifist. I wish you knew him. Then you would understand. I will tell you what upsets him most: Cruelty to children. Whenever he hears of it, he becomes totally unreasonable."

"Perhaps that's because he can never. . . ."

"Perhaps."

Klaus reached the cottage. The curtains were all drawn. A rockery covered the front garden. A washing line had been hung from the side of the cottage to a brick outhouse, with the dog kennel, an enclosed metal cage, against it. The dog announced his arrival by howling, the echoes travelling down into the valley. Klaus was indifferent. He knew how to kill a dog, even without the knife: Seize the front legs and pull them apart. That stretches the valves of the heart intolerably. . . .

He heard movement above him as he stood by the front door. A shutter was noisily unfolded, the window raised, and a man called down: "Who is there?"

"I fell off the Innsbruck train," Klaus said. "Have you a telephone?"

The man roared at the dog to silence it; it whimpered, and settled, its head lowered — as if it couldn't understand why a watchdog should be admonished for giving the alarm.

"Go away," he called down.

"I'm hurt. I hurt my back. I fell down the embankment."

"What are you — mad?"

"I told you — I fell out. I was leaning on the door, and it wasn't properly secured. I felt the catch give, and then I was out. The train didn't even stop."

"What do you want: A doctor, the police?"

"I have to make an important call."

Klaus saw the landing light come on, heard heavy footfalls on the staircase, a bolt being drawn, some shuffling, and the face of a farmer looking round the door at him, the tip of the shotgun protruding.

Stupid bastard, Klaus thought. I've only to push the door, knock him off balance as it goes back, and I'd have the knife in him five times before he got his finger back under the trigger-guard; easier than killing the dog.

"You are very kind," Klaus said. He lifted his elbows: The demonstration that he was unarmed. Then he held out the railway ticket: The proof he had been on the train. "I need the telephone. I will pay for the call."

They were in a narrow hall. The telephone was on a small table. The farmer wore pyjamas and enormous, thick bed socks, full of sown holes. He stood away, his back to the kitchen door, the shotgun cradled over his arm.

"It's a private call," Klaus said.

The man shrugged. He was staying. It was his house.

"I'm going to ring north Germany," Klaus said. "Here's twenty marks for the call — and a brandy if you've got one."

"No brandy. We don't drink."

He dialled Baden Baden, checking his watch. Almost four. The Dane wouldn't be in his office, but the switchboard would transfer the call to him. Klaus heard the ringing tone, a succession of bleeps.

"NATO cultural attache," a voice said.

That was pathetic. It was nearly as bad as the code-word Klaus was supposed to have used all the last week: Elvis Presley. It wouldn't even have fooled the dog, out there in the kennel.

"The Dane," Klaus said. There was no sense in trying to mask his voice behind a hand closed over the receiver; the hall was too short for that, the farmer too close.

"Who is speaking?"

"The official name in Ketchum, Idaho," Klaus said. "They

gave me some numbers, too, identifying numbers for this week, but I've forgotten them." Ketchum, Idaho. It was all second-rate, ill-conceived, outmoded. The tanks would sweep away the lot of it like so many dry leaves. A pause, while the telephonist consulted a list, pressed the transfer button, and dialled the Dane, wherever he was living.

The farmer looked bemused and distrustful. He had admitted a madman to his house. He was sure of that. He wondered how to get him out.

The Dane. The voice was smooth and easy, perfectly alert although he had been crudely woken from sleep; the legacy from the war, the animal ability never to be vulnerable by surrendering totally to fatigue. Klaus had acquired it, too, without a war.

"Hello," Klaus said. "Two of them on the Innsbruck train. They threw me off. The tall one I was telling you about must have found another thug from somewhere. Perhaps they have an unending supply of them. I hurt my back. I went down a ravine. They're still on the train. Tell Clark. They should get to Innsbruck soon, depending on the delay at the customs. Tell him two men, one my height, one shorter. The tall one doesn't like violence. They might get the girl and torture her, for all I know."

The Dane made no observation at first. "The American Secretary of State has resigned," he said at length, but that was only to buy himself a little time while he examined the options. "I imagined that might interest you."

"Tell Clark I'm trying to get to Innsbruck. There won't be any more trains, ever. I'll have to walk on down to the nearest place to here — it's called Degerndorf — and hire a taxi." Klaus turned, faced the farmer. "Taxis in Degerndorf, yes?" The farmer nodded. His hands remained on the shotgun.

"It's going to take some time," Klaus said. "They're not letting vehicles over any more. But if he takes me right to the frontier, maybe I can walk across and get another taxi on the Austrian side."

The Dane said: "Were you badly injured? You do seem to attract these things." He might have been an Englishman, politely enquiring about the eccentricity of another. "Are you TOO badly injured?"

Klaus said no.

They both knew it was rank untruth, too obvious to require comment or embellishment. Unfeeling, headstrong, youthful bravado, without the strength to admit weakness. That was why Klaus had been picked.

He put the receiver down, found a fifty mark note and took two or three steps towards the farmer; held out the money and — as a calloused hand stretched for it — grasped the barrel of the shotgun, half way down, and pressed it against the wall.

"Listen to me," Klaus said. Their eyes met. The farmer was a heavy man with a sagging stomach hanging over the cord which held his pyjama bottoms. He did not move. "When I go out of that door, you didn't see me. Nobody came here. Nobody knocked in the night. The dog didn't bark. Did it?"

The farmer looked away.

"Did it?"

"You're crazy."

"And if anybody asked for a description of me, and if anybody — anybody at all, even the police — asked about a telephone conversation I might have had, I wasn't here at all so I couldn't have had one, could I?"

It was agreed in silence.

"Funny thing," Klaus said. "It's nice here. I like the soil. I could come back. You might not like that." He gazed at the shotgun and released it. "An Imperial seven-double-five," he remarked, casually. "Unloaded. When you put the cartridges in, that metal clip moves automatically to the downward position. What do you think I am: A fool?" He moved towards the door. "Just go back to sleep. Thinking about sheep, or whatever you people think about. Count them. You're a farmer. It could be good practice." The bitter smile. "How far is Degerndorf?"

"Ten minutes' walk."

Clark was woken by the telephone at his bedside. The Dane was camouflaging it well, but Clark could tell he was concerned.

Klaus wandered past the dog. It stood and shook itself, held by the fear of its masters' rebuke. the instinct to howl struggling uneasily with the dimmed memory of the command word that it should not. He walked through a wooden gate and down a track carelessly laid with pebbles and stones. The cattle were on their haunches in a field, behind a stone wall, near an elaborate wooden structure to hold the hay at feeding time, twice a day. The lights of Degerndorf were as clear as the stars, and, it seemed to him, just as distant. Light years away. To be seen but never approached.

At last, Clark asked: "Where is Gorlish?"

"Why do you wish such information?"

"Curiosity."

"He is back in London." The Dane was not surprised by the question, not at all. "Since you are both English, I assume you had some sort of understanding. There can be little harm in telling you."

Clark was pleased. Maybe Major Clark wasn't such a fool after all. Nor such a bad prophet, either.

Klaus reached the railway station at four thirty-five. It was deserted. He found the telephone booth, against a wall, searched in the directory. The advertisement promised taxis day and night. He rang the number, listened to it ring out for a long time before a voice, masked by sleep and not like the Dane, answered.

"I want a taxi."

"To where?"

"Munich," Klaus lied. "The trains have finished."

"Forty five marks to Munich, after midnight."

"OK."

"Where are you?"

"At the railway station."

"Give me fifteen minutes. I have to get dressed."

The Audi came from across the square, driven by a teenager. Klaus was on the pavement and motioned towards the car as it pulled up. He clambered in, lowering himself carefully to the seat because his back was so painful, his stomach, too.

"You hurt yourself?" the teenager wondered. He was about nineteen, a fresh-faced, unspoilt kid. The taxi work would finance the car for him.

"I fell down in the ice," Klaus said. "How long to get to Innsbruck?"

"Forever," the teenager said. The radio was on, a bleak all-night music show where they put on long-playing jazz records and let them go right to the end. "They closed the frontier to all cars. They're still letting some lorries through. Anyway, you told me Munich."

"I know. The trouble is, my grandmother lives near Innsbruck and I've just remembered it's her birthday tomorrow. I promised to be there. Two hundred marks to take me, plus petrol."

"Look, I've told you, they won't let cars through. I can take you up there, but they won't even let you cross on foot. You know what Austrians are like."

"Turn that radio off, will you? That rubbish music gets on

my nerves. The words of those songs — you ever heard crap like that?" Klaus took out the money, laid it on his knee so that the teenager could see the two hundred-mark notes, and the single fifty-mark note. "Mountain roads," Klaus said. "You people — you're like goats. You can run up and down Alps. They say you're born with one leg shorter than the other, so that you can stand up straight." The teenager laughed hugely. He was beginning to like Klaus; or, at least, like his style. "Let's take a nice, quiet little sideroad over, one where the lazy Austrians haven't bothered to put up a customs post. Come on, there must be half a dozen." The teenager was looking at the money. It was almost a week's wages. He hesitated, a moment of greed pushing him to ask for 300 and the petrol money; noticed Klaus's face, said nothing.

"The roads aren't clear up there. It's been snowing for three, four days. The snowploughs don't bother with the minor roads; not in the mountains." He lifted his arm towards the circle of them. "Avalanches, when the fresh snow is still moist and begins to thaw. . . ."

Klaus took out another fifty.

The teenager gathered it all, smoothed each note and placed them all in his pig-skin wallet.

"You got chains on the wheels?"

The teenager grunted in contempt. Of course he had chains on the wheels. Who would live in Degerndorf in the winter and not have them?

The road was good as far as Bayrischzell, even though they were climbing. The border wasa bare eight kilometres away. They reached a cross-roads flanked by pine trees, and the teenager swung the Audi left, into a lane wide enough only for a single vehicle. He slowed, letting the chains cut down through the snow to the tarmac for grip.

"It gets worse up there," he said. The headlights picked out the way ahead, throwing the drifting white dunes into sharp relief. Still they climbed, and now they were on a ledge, the rockface on one side, the drop on the other. The snow was deeper and the car wheels were cutting furrows into it. On a plateau, a lay-by curved away. "They use that as a passing place," the teenager said. "In summer, when people take the scenic tour."

"If I'd wanted a guide, I'd have hired one." Klaus didn't want to talk, especially to a kid.

The teenager wasn't so sure he liked him now.

The engine was labouring, and only the low gears kept the car moving forward. They came down from the plateau and the back-end began to slide. He caught it and brought it back under control, braked softly. He had delicate hands which rested lightly on the steering-wheel. "Thank God we weren't out on one of the ledges," he said. "It's too dangerous, and you can see that for yourself. I'll have to try and turn round. You can have all the money back. I'll give it to you now."

He saw Klaus's hand move to the pocket of the flying-jacket, feel for the handle and withdraw the knife. He laid it on his knee, where the money had been.

"We go on," Klaus said.

The girl wanted to know who had telephoned. Clark told her to be quiet. He lay back on his bed.

"I was going to ask if we could have the light on," she said, "since neither of us can sleep. I thought I might read. Then I remembered I left my book in Munich. It was a library book, so I suppose I shouldn't have brought it, anyway."

"You joined a library?"

"Of course. Arthur did, too. I've explained to you that he was very well organised. We went there the first day. You know what he got a book on? Everyday Russian Phrases. It's been worrying me."

The teenager was shaken. Klaus wondered coldly if his

nerve had gone, and he'd have to drive the car himself.

The teenager was hunched over the wheel now, peering through the windscreen, searching for the road because the wind had drawn the snow across it, creating an undulating wilderness. They were high, above the tree line, and there was nothing except the rock, sometimes overhanging, and the drop. "A bus went down there three years ago," the teenager said. "It happened at night. The driver got lost and took this road by mistake. A pensioners' outing. The bus is still there. It took three days to find all the bodies. Some had been thrown out — seventy, eighty metres." The car was struggling again. "We'll never make it. We have to descend and climb again — on the other side, over there. I'll never build enough momentum to take us up. If I try and accelerate now, anything could happen." Klaus could just see the outline of the road, contorting back beyond the dip, rising sharply. The rockface screening it had been blasted smooth and vertical to create it.

The teenager said: "You must have come from Munich. The riots up there were on the news. People must be tense. A woman heard an aeroplane passing and died of a heart attack. You know what they're like in Munich: Strange people." The wind was crying against the rock, brushing snow against the windscreen. Mechanically, he turned on the wipers. "The Russians won't come," he said. "They wouldn't dare. Would they?" He turned for that instant, seeking counsel from the man from Munich, the man who would know.

Klaus said: "Just drive."

"We're over the border now. Not that it matters a damn." They had reached the incline. The road seemed utterly steep. He slipped down into first gear and just let the Audi go until it came to a halt, less than half way up and at an angle across the road. He kept the wheels spinning, but the car wouldn't move; it lurched forward once and slid back again. "That's it," he said. He was watching Klaus, praying the knife wouldn't come out. Sweat lay on his forehead. "The Austrian police will arrest me," he said, nervously suggesting that all this was Klaus's fault.

"Tell them you got lost, like the pensioners' coach, and the road was too bad to go back. Austrians are stupid. They'd probably believe that." They were standing at the rear of the car, surveying the wide grooves that the wheels had created.

"There's no house near here," the teenager said helplessly. "Nowhere to ring for help. We will have to walk."

"Walk how far?"

"Landl is maybe two kilometres."

Klaus looked at his watch. 5.40. He walked slowly. Dawn had started, the faintest arc of pale, deathly white, an almost unreal, pastel shading, between the mountain peaks.

The people from the east would select their moment. Then they'd take the girl and use her. That wouldn't be difficult. A child could trick Clark. They certainly would. Probably they wouldn't be so gentle with him, either; hustle him off a quiet pavement, up an alley, two of them, one behind, a hand over his mouth, the other in front, kicking at his stomach. It would take less than a minute and Clark would lie, behind some dustbins, like a stuck pig, crying, blood on his hands, wanting to die.

An Klaus wouldn't be there. He'd be here, in this snow, struggling forward, a step at a time, the damned, damned stuff up to his waist, cloying and clinging. He was angry enough to have attacked the rockface itself if he had had something heavy — like the car jack — to do it with.

The teenager was further back and Klaus had abandoned him; the younger man was certainly fitter, but he didn't have the stamina and he didn't have the anger.

Klaus saw Landl, lost in the pine trees. Lingering half-light, and nearly seven o'clock. He couldn't believe two kilometres had taken that long. He saw the chalet roofs heavy with snow, and smoke from a chimney; and he was going down, towards the chalets, his legs impossibly heavy, like lead clubs. The teenager hadn't appeared. Klaus hadn't even got his money back.

Clark was anxious. He stood by the lounge window, watching the station. The Munich train was due shortly because the taxis were gathering for it.

"The journey must have been a nightmare for the passengers," he said to the girl. "Over seven hours from Munich. The Austrians must have made the train wait an eternity at the frontier."

A German woman came into the lounge, breathless. She was young and beautifully groomed. She might have been a fashion model, here on an assignment. "They're forcing all foreigners to register," she said. She stood in the clearing between the chairs and sofas, beside the swing door. She'd almost lost control of herself. "We all have to go to the town hall at nine to apply for temporary resident's permits. That's what they are calling them. If they are not granted, we'll be deported." She turned from side to side, searching for a familiar face which might console her, might tell her this was not true. "They told me in a shop down the street. They're keeping lists." She abandoned herself completely, and Clark thought she was going to break down. "Where is my husband?" she pleaded. "Where are my children?"

He turned to the window again. The train had arrived, unseen, behind the wall beside the station building which butted onto a warehouse. He watched the first of the passengers come down the steps from the main hall, spreading out. They looked weary and wrecked, even from that distance. He couldn't see two men together, one short, the other exactly the height of Klaus.

Klaus knocked at a door. A woman opened it. Two

children were eating breakfast from a log cabin in the kitchen. "I need a taxi," he said.

"Down the road," she replied. She was suspicious. Where had this man been during the night, and how had he got here? "It's not a real taxi, it's just a man who hires his car." Aren't they all, Klaus thought, aren't they all? "His name is Herr Habicht. His house is next to the church."

The police came in a white Volkswagen van, with an insignia painted on the side, a coat of arms. They wore uniforms which were almost black, and that made them seem more numerous, an army of the night. They anticipated hostility. As they came singly through the swing door, they spread out in a line, hands behind their backs: The classic position. The customs officials had adopted it, too. One of them, who had a golden star at the tip of each shoulder, positioned himself in the front.

"The burgermeister, on the instructions of the Government of the Austrian Republic, has decreed that all aliens report to the town hall at nine o'clock to apply for permits to remain in Austria. The town hall is situated in Maria Theresien Strasse. When you arrive there, you will form an orderly queue." As he spoke, one of the policemen broke away and walked stiffly to the reception desk. The visitors book was offered to him, and he began to copy all the names onto a notepad. "There will be a six o'clock curfew each evening, beginning today. Anyone breaking it will be subject to imprisonment and deportation, whether they have a permit or not."

"Cowards," the old woman taunted them. "I gave two sons in 1942. . . ."

The policeman looked straight at her.

How many times had this happened, thirty years ago, Clark wondered: The obedient German soldiers in heavy boots, ruling without discussion; wielding the all-embracing power without the consequences of it; applying it equally to the aged and the infirm, the women and children. No questions permitted. The orders are the orders. Moses himself might have created them, etched into tablets of stone, and a thousand years would not wear them away. And now it was happening to the Germans.

"The Russians will come here anyway," the woman said.

A movement outside attracted Clark's eye. There was a man in a doorway, a tall man, thin, even with a winter coat on. He was looking vaguely towards the hotel, watching the door in case anybody came out.

Klaus walked down the sloping street towards the church, saw the only house near it — a modern bungalow with an angled roof and scenic garden — and knocked on the door. A woman in an overall appeared, bare, white legs and worn-out carpet slippers.

"Herr Habicht, please" Klaus said quietly. He was feeling tired.

"One moment." She called back, into the darkened interior of the chalet: "Hermann!"

Habicht was unkempt and unattractive; fifty and gone to seed. He wore a soiled shirt, the sleeves rolled up. He hadn't bothered to shave; probably not for a couple of days.

"Innsbruck," Klaus said.

"Sure. 350 schillings."

"I'm paying in marks."

"People around here aren't so keen on them any more."

"I heard. I read the newspapers, too."

"A hundred marks."

"Fifty."

"Seventy-five."

"All right. But there's a condition. I want to be there within the hour."

Habicht closed the door, leaving Klaus on the step; returned wearing an old, pea-green sports jacket and holding the car keys. "The car is in the garage down there," and he pointed to a shed in an orchard, flanked by hen coops. "Fifty-five minutes to Innsbruck. An hour, more like. They're making all foreigners register down there, even Germans. You know that?"

The policeman continued the rehearsed speech, his fourth or fifth time this morning. "The town hall is opening specially early. All aliens will remain in their hotels until nine o'clock. Then you will make your way in a calm and orderly fashion to the town hall." The speech was over. He looked to see how the man copying the names was faring; received a nod; and just stood.

The hotel manager had appeared from down a corridor and stood away, unsure of what to do. He was a small, urgent, bird-like man in a dark, striped suit with thinning, greying hair who had spent — as he had a habit of assuring guests — twenty years building up a reputation for cleanliness and decency and friendliness, especially among foreign visitors. His cramped office was full of the postcards they had sent him from many places — Japan, California, Brazil. All that was over. He surveyed the silent room, for the first time unsure of his place in it and whether it had been completely usurped; his own lounge held in artificial silence, compounded of resentment and fear.

"We're untried prisoners in a free country." The old woman again. Her walking stick vibrated at her side. "You daren't even try us. Cowards, cowards, cowards. . . ."

The manager rubbed his hands together urgently.

The autobahn was only seven kilometres away. They joined it at Kufstein, the mountains suddenly far back from the road on both sides. Klaus had closed his eyes. Habicht hadn't told him it wasn't a car. He hadn't told him it was an open-backed Ford transit van, the rear compartment strewn with decaying hay. A farm vehicle for transporting pigs to market. Never mind. It did a steady 90 kph, just the legal speed, and it was going to Innsbruck.

When the police had withdrawn — through the swing door and over the road to the hotel opposite — Clark looked at the time. 8.20. He sat down. Forty minutes to kill. The figure in the doorway was still there, occasionally shifting the weight of his body from one foot to the other.

8.25 The girl was beside him. They had exhausted all conversation long ago, and not even the dried-up remnants of their relationship held them together; only the circumstances.

8.30 A page boy in uniform came in through the swing door, holding an envelope. He went to the reception desk, spoke inaudibly to the girl there, left the envelope and departed. She rose, searching among the seventy or eighty people in the lounge; located Clark, walked over, smiled pleasantly, and gave the envelope to him.

"Where did the boy come from?" he asked.

"I don't know. He didn't say."

The envelope had no name on it. It was fawn-coloured, the back stiff because it was re-inforced by cardboard. He opened it with the nail of his thumb and took out the single piece of paper.

The girl was disinterested. She was looking vacantly out of the window, across the square to the station. The snow had begun again, a few lazy flakes descending as slowly as autumn leaves.

The tall man had retreated further into the doorway to avoid it.

Clark twisted in his chair so that he was facing the girl, and she couldn't see the side of the paper on which were written fifteen lines of longhand, in ink, in sloping, careful handwriting, with a wide margin at each side.

Eindhoven. Personnel: 3, 2 male, 1 female. Base: 17,

Hoofdweg. Group leader: Grott, Anton. Primary code-name: Lowlander. Secondary code-name: Sea Pigeon. Code number: H/1/1. Code series: Western Division. Fall-back base: Hapert. Issued with: 7 Armalite rifles 8/4/75, 2 Webley revolvers 8/4/75. (Memorandum: The greasing requires inspection on or before 8/4/80.) 14 NATO max-impact grenades. Issued 53 kg food in sealed containers, to be consumed or replaced 13/9/82. Issued 3 K16 fall-out masks (Memorandum: The tubes and cylinders require inspection on or before 1/1/79). Primary targets: Markelo chemical plant, Helmond; the span bridge over autobahn E3, 2.3 km south of Eindhoven; if civil agitation, discretion to be used. Group status: OK.

When he had fininshed reading it, Clark folded the piece of paper and placed it in his wallet. He was not at all sure what the legend meant. Eindhoven? That was in southern Holland. He'd think about the rest of it later.

The tall man had gone.

The girl said distantly: "Anything important?"

"I don't know." It was then, just then, when the snow was heavier and the cloud lower, and the purity of the dawn had been turned into a spoilt, flawed, colourless day, that he understood. Dahlem had sent the piece of paper. Dahlem had found a page boy, given him a heavy tip, and told him to deliver it. The people from the east were watching Clark. Dahlem would know that. He'd have seen them for himself. They'd see Clark get the envelope and think it was the exchange. They'd think he had all the pieces of paper now. They'd move for him.

The bastard, he murmured, to himself. The girl watched him in curiosity. Dahlem had used them in the cemetery, to get Klaus. Now he was using them again.

Clever. Everybody said Dahlem was clever. Or

calculating, at least. . . .

Clark looked again at the empty doorway. Sure the tall man had gone. He'd consult the other, report the arrival of the envelope, plan the move. Maybe at this moment they were in a cafe, with a street-map spread before them, and a nicotine-stained finger was tracing the route from the hotel to Maria Theresien Strasse, hesitating at the strategic points — the alleys and cross-roads — and talking quietly in German.

8.42. Clark said to the girl: "We must leave for the town hall in eight minutes. When we do, you will walk close by my side. Understood?"

"Why are you saying this?"

But his thoughts had drifted away. What did the words on the paper mean?

They were at Jenbach, and the mountains were closing on the road again. The stark, rugged peaks pressed down on them; higher up, mist had gathered, static, blending against the threadbare snow. Klaus opened his eyes to check the time. Going on nine. They'd be there in twenty minutes. Habicht's arms were locked onto the steering wheel like rods. He sat erect, his back away from the seat, looking straight ahead. He was a solid driver, no delicacy of touch at all. Klaus wondered how the teenager would rescue the Audi.

"We must leave now," Clark said. Others in the lounge were rising, talking among themselves, putting on coats, searching for missing gloves. A few had left already, even though they were early.

The manager was by the swing door, trying to redeem everything. "Tonight," he said despairingly, "we will have a special dinner and it will be free. I will find a real Tyrolean band everybody can dance!"

But they ignored him. The moment was wrong and, if he sensed that, the impulses of atonement were too strong. They filed past him, looking away, finding his presence an embarrassment; out onto the pavement, right, and they tramped down Museumstrasse.

Clark felt the cold air against his skin when he emerged. The square was almost empty. He looked round. Nobody. Nobody, but the human procession, the women in lunar boots, the children in anoraks, in knots and groups, spread back, moving at a slow march, heads down, into the snow. Marktgraben, where Museumstrasse joined the curving arterial road, and the procession thickened as it was fed by other hotels. A few locals were on the corner, observing the event and not quite understanding why it was happening; they had come out, as peasants will come out, in rural villages, to look at traffic jams.

The girl did stay close to him. At each footstep, he anticipated the move. He had no delusions that they would be inhibited, just because it was in public. If it came to a fight, or even a struggle, the procession would divert, mutely, from it and pass by on the other side. No foreigner would want trouble; and most of all, not here and not now.

"You're nervous," the girl said. "You're looking round all the time."

They followed Marktgraben for fifty yards and Maria Theresien Strasse was on the left, a wide boulevard. The procession was streaming across it, regardless of the traffic — that had halted — and had reached the far pavement.

Like Kaesong, he thought, just like Kaesong; just this pace, just these groupings, just this subdued confusion, just this uncertainty.

The town hall was a gaunt, Gothic building of reddish stone slabs; an edifice, almost a monument. Alcoves had been shaped into the slabs far up and religious figurines placed there, the fresh snow at their feet; the roof was a series of cupolas, with two television aerials between them, clipped to the tiles. Clark gazed at it all from the end of the queue, a

hundred and fifty yards away. The door was a stone arch
with smooth stones for steps. Above it, a circular mural had
been painted onto the brickwork: A nativity scene. But some
of the paint had worn away, and the picture was fragmented.

They stood, themselves, in the snow, three and four deep in
their coats, like cattle; prisoners of no war, moving slowly
forward at intervals and at a speed determined by others. A
newspaper seller worked his way along them, the papers in
the crook of his arm, calling his wares: Emergency measures!
Emergency measures!

Clark scanned the street. The Austrians were keeping
away from the queue, here, staying on the other pavement in
their dark fur hats, going silently about their business. It was
Monday, after all: The start of the week. Back down the
street, a cream-coloured caravan had been towed to a
position at the kerbside, a flap in its side lifted, and a youth
had begun to sell hamburgers. The caravan had come to
service the queue. The word was spreading. Of course.
They'd still want to make money out of the foreigners.

The odour of frying onions drifted on the wind.

Clark's eyes were moving past the tide of people in front of
him, to the curve in the road and the traffic lights.

Still nothing.

Klaus was awake. He saw the blue roadsign:

> Wattens 2 km
> Innsbruck 15 km
> Matrei 36 km
> Brenner Pass 43 km.

but chalk had been drawn through the bottom line, and a
message daubed in black on a makeshift board laid at the
base of the roadsign: The Brenner Pass is closed to all motor
traffic indefinitely.

Habicht said: "It was the Italians. They closed it first. We would have done, but they were quicker." They both smiled. "They're even more frightened than we are." His eyes never left the level autobahn which was going easily down into the valley. "People say things are bad over there. Since the communists came. No fresh fruit, no nylons, the phones don't work anymore. There was a riot in Bolsano about bread prices, but they hushed all that up." He was an ordinary man, dealing in rumour and dull reflection. "The Italians are cowboys, especially on the Brenner," he said. "They shot a Turkish lorry driver who tried to get across last week. They fired a cannon at his lorry!" He fumbled in his pocket for a cigarette from a paper pack. "No fresh fruit," he repeated, almost a murmur, to himself. "Our turn next."

The queue had moved a little. Clark was in line with a sports goods shop, the window an armoury of upturned skis and ski poles and helmets on ledges, and bogus white flakes, imitating snow, scattered across green beige platforms, and a poster of a downhill racer with a slogan beside it: Willie Kurt uses Wisdom skis! And, in much smaller type: Criterium de la Premiere Neige, Val d'Isere, France, 1976. But that was before the communists.

It was cold; a different sort of cold to Munich. There, in the city, it had been a damp, chilled, moist glove which rubbed against the skin; here, the air was dry, the fingers of the glove frozen together.

"The papers," Clark said. His elbow rested against the point where the wallet protruded. The single sheet which Dahlem had sent was there. "Tell me about the papers."

"We've been through all this so many times before," she said. He arms were folded across her chest, trying to nurture a little warmth. Her toes were already numb. "Why do you keep on asking me? I saw one or two, but they didn't mean anything. Just numbers. What do you expect me to have done: De-code them myself? I was a typist with a firm of accountants." Her head moved away from him in contrived disgust.

The snow had melted into his hair, leaving it sodden; impatiently he brushed a hand back through it, dried the hand against his handkerchief; and they shuffled forward a few paces again.

He saw the tall man come, away beyond the caravan and the few customers in front of it. He was leaning against a wall between two shops. He must have calculated he was too far away to be recognised.

The slip road descended sharply and looped back under the autobahn. The road passed the rim of an industrial estate, and they were into older, detached houses, in an avenue of trees planted with the regularity and spacing of lampposts.

9.30.

"Where do you want to go?"

"The railway station."

A single bell tolling marked the half hour; a bell in an unseen belfry, lost somewhere in the falling snow and the slanting rooftops. It tolled just once, a deep, vibrant, guttural sound; echoed, and was silent.

The rumour passed back, mouth to mouth, like a current: They were going to close the town hall doors at any moment. An official had calculated a resident's quota for Innsbruck, to accord with the health regulations. It was almost filled.

Two police vans — again the white, again the coats of arms — threaded through the cars at the far end of the street, drew up opposite the town hall, and twenty policemen climbed out. They wore fur-lined, black, leather jackets and black boots. They formed into fours and began to patrol the queue, each squad with its own territory. The batons were at their wrists, held there by straps.

At the other end of the street, an army lorry rounded the corner very slowly and was positioned behind a bollard midway between the pavements; a squat, ungainly, khaki vehicle, its bonnet shaped like a snout, resting on huge tyres, and camouflage netting clinging to the walls of the rear compartment.

The traffic was being directed away.

Klaus paid the man when they reached the railway station, then walked quickly over to the hotel. He'd experienced this before, and if he didn't understand it, it worked: Fatigue accentuated all pain to a certain point, but dulled it after that. It was true that his back ached, but that was no more than an abstract inconvenience now. But his eyes were red and livid from the lack of sleep. He'd told Habicht not to light the cigarette, because of what the smoke would do to them. Habicht had refused, and that was why he hadn't got a tip.

They were within sight of the oaken doors, the hewn wood shaped to fit beneath the arches. An old knocker, a metal hoop, hung from one of the doors. The queue was up the steps, feeding into the building and two policemen, batons held waist-high and horizontal to the ground, were letting people in two at a time, at signals from within.

The tall man had moved a little closer, keeping just 50 yards away from Clark. He stood erect, hands in his pockets. He was waiting his time; waiting until Clark and the girl had been in, got their permits, and were coming back. That would be the moment.

Klaus was at the reception desk. The girl explained what was happening and gave him the simple directions to Maria Theresien Strasse.

"How far?"

"On foot — ten minutes. Of course I don't know how fast you can walk."

If the circumstances had been different, he would have

interpreted the coy smile as a come-on. She must have liked the pock-marks on his face.

Some of the guests had already returned and sat in the lounge. One held his permit; inspected it with distaste. He was an elderly man with wisps of white hair and a face of great gentility; a gentleman, you would say, a former officer and now a gentleman. But you've seen all this before, Klaus thought. You couldn't have avoided the war. You established the precedent. You've seen the innocent ones, trying to read and understand their permits. It might have been in Kharkov, or Oslo, or Lyons, or Warsaw. . . .

He went into Museumstrasse. More were coming back. A woman had been sobbing, but that was because she'd got a permit.

Twenty people remained between Clark and the doors. The girl had almost nestled into him and complained — a whining, artificially pitched noise, created to be an irritant — constantly about the cold.

They both heard the order: "Nein! Nein!"

It could have been an Austrian or a German, policeman or civilian. The doors were being pushed laboriously closed. A voice over a megaphone began: "Disperse quietly. The allocation of permits has terminated. No further permits will be issued, even in cases of hardship. Return to your hotels. . . ."

But the people on the steps had bunched and were pressing at the doors. A policeman raised his baton but was engulfed, his back forced against the stone arch. And the doors were back, wide and open; and the queue broke, in the snow; disintegrated into a mob. Clark saw a child brushed aside, almost knocked down; an aged woman, trapped between two men, crying for mercy; and the mob was at the gates, in a ragged, seething circle from it out onto the road, jostling and pushing to get through. The woman went down, slithering between the bodies, and was dragged forward, her skirt drawn up to her narrow thighs, one hand over her face.

The police were plucking at the edge of the mob, grasping people, dragging them out. One of the vans was being backed up, its rear doors open, more police inside, handcuffs on hooks.

A baton was wielded, and three Germans flooded at a lone policeman. A woman was trying to claw him from behind, her handbag fallen into the snow and abandoned, her hair in her eyes, her leg bleeding.

He heard the voice over the megaphone: "Recht und ordnung! Recht und ordnung!" Then that went silent; silent as the church bell.

He heard a whistle, and the clatter of military boots along the pavement. The soldiers were coming. They formed a wedge and tried to bore a path into the shifting, contorting mob, their arms locked together. He saw somebody spit at them, and a fist go deep into a young soldiers' stomach; but the soldier couldn't double up because of the arms holding him at each side. He heard the child shrieking, and a German calling out: "Kill them all."

The girl had ebbed from him, carried on the current; her head was bobbing twenty feet away, towards the road, dipping and rising, like a swimmer struggling to keep above water; and he was held by the body of the mob, almost under the arch. She reached the edge, where the fighting was going on, detached herself and ran, never turning, into a gap between the last of the soldiers and two policemen; went through it and on, into the ebbing curtain of snow.

The tall man tensed, removed his hands from his pockets and watched the girl pass on the other pavement; Clark had turned himself round and was threshing with his elbows and knees against the current.

The tall man wasn't interested in the girl. He wanted Clark. He thought the exchange had been completed. He thought

Clark had all the papers. . . .

Dahlem had calculated that.

Clark felt a hand trying to hold him back, a useless hand, with no strength, clinging to the collar of his coat; ducked his head and the hand was released; felt heavy bodies battering against him, and a head against his chest, the hair smelling of cheap lotion; but he was going forward.

The girl was at the traffic lights when he was free, running slowly. She wore ordinary boots, the soles unsuited to snow, and particularly snow which had been trampled into ice.

A policeman was close to him. Their eyes came together in barbaric communion. Clark waited for the baton; but a German lurched between them and began to abuse the policeman.

Clark was free, free of the after-birth. He started to run. The hamburger caravan had closed, fearing a seige. He drew level with it, and the tall man, still ahead, moved.

The width of the wide road lay between them.

But Clark could still run. He was fit, a bloody sight fitter than most; he'd do an assault course in even time, tunnels, water jumps, ropes from trees, the lot. But he wondered if he could outrun the tall man, now in his wake.

The girl had turned into Herzog Strasse, a narrow street and now, at this moment, an empty street because the riot had driven the people indoors, fearing the bigger siege; and the rampage, and the looting. There could have been 200,000 Germans out there.

Bastard. Clark taunted himself. Breath was coming hard, and his lungs felt constricted. Bastard. Dahlem got a message to her in the hotel, telling her when to run; got it delivered while I was in the toilet, while I was. . . .

When he turned, his right foot slid, like a vehicle, in making the turn; and he lost his balance, floundered, ended almost crouching; ran on.

An empty street. No witnesses, not one. The man could

shoot him in the back of the neck, search him and melt into the side streets; but he'd have to stop to fire and, in the act of stopping, Clark would have increased the distance between them. He'd be out of range, unless a chance shot got him. Like Echtmann. Just like Echtmann.

He heard many discordant voices then, from life and from the grave, in a kind of rising chorus, and one of them was a cold, precise, English voice, detached from the others and above them: Echtmann ran directly at the wire. Was he not briefed? Was he not. . . .?

And Clark began to zig-zag, even if that was probably the stupidest thing he could have done on ice.

An alley, a corridor between two walls; thirty feet long, and a building over the end of it, making it into a tunnel; a cobbled rectangle, and tall, deserted, ruined houses on all sides, decayed, windowless, the backs of the roofs broken; masonry and timber fallen; tall houses, tall enough to preclude daylight, side by side, holding each other up. Some had begun to lean, despite the support. An old clockface was opposite him, on a wall. The ornate hands had stopped at precisely twenty-two minutes past three.

He was in the rectangle, turning and turning, searching for her footmarks in the snow.

The tall man halted, breathless, at the end of the alley and watched him. They were thirty feet apart; perhaps a little less. Clark noted mechanically the make of the revolver: Belgian. A NATO weapon, standard issue. To be safe, when they dug the bullets out for the autopsy. He'd used the Czech rifle for Echtmann, for the same reason. The same stinking logic, looking beyond the kill.

He closed his eyes.

When he opened them, the man was in front of him. They were almost in the shadow of the houses. The man lifted the thick barrel of the revolver and struck him the face. As Clark went back, he felt it strike him again, across the forehead. He saw the snow as if it was coming up around him and he was falling, falling deep into it. The third blow — swung from far away — was against the back of his head.

He saw Klaus behind the man: Klaus, lungs heaving for breath, the left hand trembling, the right holding the knife, hair dishevelled from the running, eyes enraged.

He heard the knife go in as the left arm locked around the man's neck, a slicing, a whispering, the most terrible sound that he had ever heard; saw the man buckle at the knees, hands trying to reach his own back, cough as if he were choking, and fall forward.

There's another man, Clark tried to say. A second man. The short one. Two of them. But his lips would not form sentences or phrases or even stupid, single words.

He heard the shot — it seemed to come from the direction of the alley. It would have done. It echoed through the wrecked tenements. And he couldn't see Klaus any more.

A Belgian revolver, he thought. In the sub-conscious, he thought, all evaluations are instinctive, however repellent, however inapt.

And he hated himself.

AFTERNOON

A room, a bare room; the wallpaper had peeled and green patterns of mildew clung to the exposed plaster behind it. A campbed against one wall, with a grey blanket neatly lain over it and a hand towel, folded into a small square, placed at the end of it. The curtains were drawn because the window panes were broken. Shattered crockery lay in a corner; dust had settled in a thick scum on it.

One of the tenement houses.

Clark was on floorboards. The pillow had been removed from the bed and pushed under his head.

His eyes would not focus properly, no matter how hard he tried. The mountain mist seemed to have penetrated them.

He heard the girl, soft and remote. "The police have been and gone away. They didn't find us." Naturally. They wouldn't have spent too much time searching, not with 200,000 Germans out there....

He tried to turn but his strength and his co-ordination had gone; and he lay still again, on his back, his hands by his sides.

Dahlem was in the room.

"Your friend," the girl said, and he saw the outline of her arm motion towards the window, and the rectangle below. "I'm sorry." Klaus was dead.

"We're going away soon," she said. "We'll ring the police and tell them where you are. It was very difficult bringing you up here. You could hardly walk at all. You almost fell several times." She was composed.

Dahlem said suddenly: "I've been listening to the radio all day." He had a tiny, Japanese transistor in his hand. "It's too late." He wore a blue suit. He placed the radio on the bed. "It's today." He had switched the radio on. Thin, metallic music. He came close to Clark and stopped. "I did not want to have to arrange to for you and the other people to destroy each other." His voice was thin — the same as the radio; the mincing level of the eunuch and the queer.

"All violence is shocking. But you obliged me. Didn't you believe I was able to set that up?" He was flaunting his own damn intelligence.

And the girl said: "Arthur, don't be hard with him, it wasn't his fault, he helped me in the cemetery...."

"I know. That is the only reason I agreed to bring him up here."

Dahlem was at the window. "Some blood remains on the snow. I expect they will leave that." Clark could picture him, through the mist. The short hair, the thick lenses of the spectacles. Still the music continued. "The papers," he said. "She tells me you were not even informed of their contents. I find that most puzzling." He discussed it as if it were an academic question which faintly interested him. Probably he was like that with everything. He released the curtain. "Do you wish to know the contents?"

Clark moved his head. This was Dahlem's moment: The moment when he saw the power he had, not as a plan or a discordant voice over a telephone, arranging an exchange; not as a series of clinical numbers and codes, passing across his desk; but real.

"We will lose the war," Dahlem said. "This has long been accepted, though never admitted. Partly it was lack of funds. Partly it was will. Perhaps the two factors come together somewhere. All the planning was directed at what would happen when we had lost. Do I surprise you? You seem that kind. They are very pragmatic in Brussels. They were very pragmatic in Brussels. It is Baden Baden now."

"What does this mean, Arthur?"

"They organised a revolution, to begin when the Russians were trying to police all Europe, from Norway to Spain. . . ." He lost himself in the contemplation; perhaps of the rainy Tuesday afternoons, when he had copied the papers. "One of their psychologists calculated that it would be necessary to hesitate for a certain time, a stated time; and that time was three weeks and four days, after the tanks had passed. It was necessary to allow the ordinary populace — their phrase — to recover because they would be disorientated and frightened at first; to start to feel resentment; and utilise this before the occupation had been completely accomplished: When the organisation of the occupiers was tenuous and uncertain; not just the sentry on the street corner, but the whole organisation."

"Arthur, this is not true."

He ignored that. "It is much better than that. I had not thought anyone in Brussels capable of such original thought. I was surprised at first. Once the revolution began, it would spread back into the satellites, East Germany, Poland, Hungary. . . and then into Mother Russia itself. When the Russians were billeted in Prague in 1968, they wouldn't let the soldiers leave their barracks in case they were contaminated by ideas. But they could never police all Europe and escape the contamination. Not if a revolution, a convulsion, a civilian convulsion, was going on." He moved away from the window. "The concept of spreading revolution is not original. Marx and Lenin both preached it. I hope you like the Brussels way of inverting the theory." He came to the place where Clark lay. "The papers are details of the groups who will launch the revolution. When the tanks have passed. Full details. Names, addresses. Some of their professions are instructive: Doctors, lawyers, trade union officials. . ."

The girl sat on the bed.

Clark thought: Three weeks and four days. He closed his eyes completely and heard, down all the years, the slap-slap of naked feet on the brown earth, the emptiness which a tank assault left, fatally and inescapably, behind it; the wreckage and the ruins and the exhaustion. A Korean priest had told him, once: When the war is over, we shall create from dust, and build our Jerusalem of mud and wattle and straw. You will see.

But it had taken partition, and fifteen years of aid. . . .

The music stopped in mid-flow. The announcer said: "In a few moments, we are bringing you a special message from the Chancellor of the Federal Republic."

Dahlem told the girl to go away and buy soup for Clark; told her to get the shop to heat it, and he could drink it straight from the tin.

When she had gone, Dahlem came very close to Clark. "You know why I chose the cemetery in Munich? Because my father is buried there." He moved, through the misty margins of Clark's vision. "He is buried very near the pond." Then: "The Dane did say you were solid. I think that was a reference to your physical attributes, not your mental." Clark, Major Clark risen through the ranks, because there was nobody to help him; he'd fashioned his career with his own bare hands, and he'd got as far as major. Why did they want to keep denigrating him? "The Dane," Dahlem went on, "is the man I admire most. He is not a man I would care to work against." He surveyed Clark; surveyed the beaten head, the caked blood dry in the hair. "Still you do not see it. That is why they picked you." He moved again. "The girl knows nothing. She believes. By the way, there are 193 names on the papers. I traded them this afternoon, at three o'clock. At the railway station. It was all very civilised. They paid money."

"Why did they pick Klaus?" The words were forced and uncertain. Clark felt pain in his throat as he spoke them.

"Too headstrong to see it. Not like you. You're too trusting."

The girl came back.

"Authenticity," Dahlem concluded, sure that she would deduce nothing of what had been said in her absence. "The Dane demanded authenticity. 193 names. That would take some checking, some bogus, entirely bogus, just enough of them authentic. That would occupy a police force when they might be doing other things."

They'd been buying a little time, after the tanks had gone. That was all.

"The Dane is most concerned about your immediate welfare."

"He should have thought about Klaus, and his welfare."

"Still you don't see it. So many will die, and because you happen to know one of them, you elevate him and apply the morality to him. The Dane disapproves of this. Some call the application the Christian ethic, but it does not stop tanks. It allows them free passage; and that is why I regard the Dane as I do."

No roll of drums, no anthem, simply a heavy, matured man pausing — pausing because the prepared statement seemed, just then inadequate; but it was all he had. "My fellow citizens, this is the Chancellor of the Federal Republic. At twelve o'clock, troops of the Warsaw Pact penetrated into West Berlin in a concentric movement...."

The girl was shaking her head slowly. Clark sensed she was going to cry.

"... without any formal notification ..."

Klaus had been sacrificed for the authenticity. To make them believe it in the east, believe the papers were real, so real they would send people to perish for them in Brussels. Nobody in the east would contradict that; nobody would doubt it. The Dane understood that. Clark wondered how many files those lean fingers had turned, hour after hour, until he had come upon himself: The perfect candidate for the hollow pursuit. Clark hadn't doubted the authenticity, either.

Dahlem gathered the girl in his arms. It was true. She knew nothing. He whispered something to her. Clark did not see them go. He heard their descending footsteps on the wooden staircase, heard them close the broken front door carefully behind them. He did not see them cross the rectangular square, Dahlem guiding the girl away from where the blood still lay; hand in hand, back down the corridor between the buildings, gone to wherever lovers go.

"And are claiming their actions are legal in international law, because of the status of Berlin, and the four-powered Allied control. . . ."

If it comforts you, the grass will grow on the bombsites and the children will play with rag balls among the broken masonry.

". . . no active resistance because the Mayor of West Berlin, after immediate consultation with the Federal Government, decreed, correctly, that resistance would only bring needless slaughter to women and children. . . ."

The Korean priest had been killed, two days after he had spoken to Clark. A random sniper's bullet, some said. Others said he'd been crushed under a tank, trying to make the driver turn back.

Jerusalem.

He thought of Joanne.